P9-ASL-497

# Southeast Asia Today—
# And Tomorrow

# SOUTHEAST ASIA TODAY—
# AND TOMORROW

## A Political Analysis

RICHARD BUTWELL

FREDERICK A. PRAEGER, *Publisher*

New York

FERNALD LIBRARY
COLBY JUNIOR COLLEGE
NEW LONDON, NEW HAMPSHIRE

JQ
96
B8

BOOKS THAT MATTER

Published in the United States of America in 1961 by
Frederick A. Praeger, Inc., Publisher
64 University Place, New York 3, N. Y.

© 1961 by Frederick A. Praeger, Inc.

All rights reserved

Library of Congress Catalog Card Number: 61-10525

SOUTHEAST ASIA TODAY—AND TOMORROW
is published in two editions:

A Praeger Paperback (PPS-60)
A clothbound edition

43861

Manufactured in the United States of America

FERNALD LIBRARY
COLBY JUNIOR COLLEGE
NEW LONDON, NEW HAMPSHIRE

# CONTENTS

# PREFACE

Two COMPARATIVELY little-known lands, the Congo in Africa and Laos in Southeast Asia, attracted world-wide attention at the start of the 1960's as key areas of conflict in the continuing Cold War between the United States and the Soviet Union. Both lands seemed on the edge of anarchy, and some "realists" among the political observers wrote them off as helpless—and hopeless—to resist the divisive subversive techniques and revolutionary appeal of international Communism. Although the pessimistic predictions about the future of both lands may prove correct, they have seemed only too frequently to proceed from hysteria rather than knowledge of the political factors at work in the two countries.

The Congo was only one of many African nations to join the ranks of the newly independent countries of the world. The late 1950's and early 1960's saw the number of the world's countries appreciably increased with the ending of colonial rule in nearly two dozen African lands. A new era was dawning for Africa—and for the world.

A comparable era had characterized Southeast Asia a decade earlier, a fact that seemed more frequently than not to be ignored as outsiders sought to understand the course of the political evolution of the new African nations. Indeed, as Africans were gaining their independence, many Southeast Asian leaders were changing their minds concerning the most appropriate governmental arrangements and policies for their lands—which suggested to me that it might be profitable to examine the character of these changes, in order to understand not only Southeast Asia but also other recently independent areas of the world.

This book was written at the same time that civil war gripped Laos in late 1960 and early 1961; it was completed at the time of Vice President Lyndon B. Johnson's return from his much-publicized mission to Southeast Asia in May, 1961. Both events suggested that the situation in Southeast Asia was still far from stabilized, with important new departures likely in the character of the Communist challenge to the area and in the American response.

When I first visited Southeast Asia in 1953, democracy's champions there were both numerous and outspoken, there was as yet no formally recognized Communist government in the region, only four countries were fully independent, and nowhere except in Thailand was the military particularly important politically. In traveling throughout Southeast Asia in 1959 and 1960, I was struck by the decline in enthusiasm for democratic government, the growth in political importance of armies, and the despair that seemed in many countries to have replaced the excitement of the early post-independence years. Moreover, there was now a Communist country in the region, one that was more than half a decade old: North Vietnam. And Laos, as it subsequently turned out, was moving closer to Communist domination.

I was fortunate to have been in Burma in February, 1960, at the time of the elections held to select civilian leaders to take over the government following the voluntary relinquishment of authority by the soldier group that had seized power eighteen months earlier. That Burma should be setting out again in pursuit of effective democratic government was an inspiring demonstration of the appeal of democracy at least for U Nu and some Burmese. However, the return of civilian rule again raised the question of whether democratic government is, in fact, appropriate for Burma—indeed, for all Southeast Asia and for the rest of the recently colonial world—at this time.

This book does not purport to give a definitive answer to this question—or to the question of the most appropriate form of economic organization for the Southeast Asian lands. It does, however, examine the experiences in the first years of independence of several Southeast Asian lands with institutions that were democratic in form, as well as those of other countries that chose different paths of political development. The book also treats the changes that have occurred in governmental forms and political institutions since independence, evolving economic and social policies, the nature of the Communist challenge, and the pattern of relations with other nations.

My primary purpose is to describe and assess the record of the lands of Southeast Asia in governing themselves after a decade of independence; to offer some suggestions, based on this examination, concerning the nature of government in this part of the world; and to chart the probable course of future development. It is hoped that this effort will contribute to an understanding of these lands and of the problems they pose for American foreign policy.

Much of the material presented in this volume is based on my reading through the years of various works by others. Accordingly, I would like to acknowledge my debt to the authors of the many specialized volumes I have read before and during the preparation of this manuscript. I would also like to acknowledge my debt to those who read the manuscript in preliminary form and made helpful suggestions, particularly Dean Amry Vandenbosch of the William Andrew Patterson School of Diplomacy and International Commerce, University of Kentucky. Others who read parts of the manuscript and offered invaluable criticism included Professors John F. Cady and Willard H. Elsbree, of Ohio University; Claude A. Buss, of Stanford University; Russell Fifield, of the University of Michigan; Lucian W. Pye, of the Massachusetts Institute of Technology; Fred von der Mehden, of the University of Wisconsin; Gerald Maryanov, of the State University of Iowa; J. Norman Parmer, of Northern Illinois University; M. Ladd Thomas, of Rutgers University; Justus M. van der Kroef, of the University of Bridgeport; H. M. Jacobini, of Southern Illinois University; Bernard B. Fall, of Howard University; and Charles B. Hagan, Phillip Monypenny, Robert E. Scott, Francis G. Wilson, and Robert Crawford, of the University of Illinois. The author, of course, accepts full responsibility for all errors of fact or judgment.

Some of the information included in this book was gathered during a 1959-60 trip to Southeast Asia, and I would like to acknowledge my gratitude for assistance received as a Fulbright Professor at the University of Rangoon from the School of

Advanced International Studies of the Johns Hopkins University and the University Research Board of the University of Illinois. Mr. Tai Hung-chao, research assistant in the Department of Political Science at the University of Illinois, also provided invaluable help. Finally, I would like to acknowledge the continuing support and assistance of my wife, Ruth, and—in his own inimitable way—of my young son, John.

R. B.

*University of Illinois*
*May 25, 1961*

# Southeast Asia Today—
# And Tomorrow

ORMOSA

# SOUTHEAST
# ASIA

PHILIPPINES

PACIFIC OCEAN

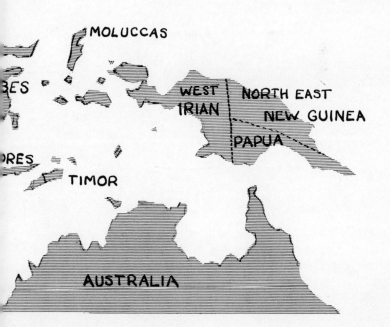

MOLUCCAS

ES

WEST
IRIAN

NORTH EAST
NEW GUINEA

PAPUA

RES

TIMOR

AUSTRALIA

# ONE

# YESTERDAY TO TODAY: ASIAN
# ROOTS AND EUROPEAN INFLUENCE

A SPIRITED young captain in the Burmese Army was a student of mine at the University of Rangoon during the 1959-60 academic year. At thirty-five, he was old enough to be disappointed with the first years of Burmese independence, but sufficiently young to hope that many of the dreams of Burmese nationalism could still be realized in his lifetime.

"I think I was about twelve when I first became aware of Burmese nationalism," he told me. "It was in the late thirties, before the Japanese occupation. My older brother was active in the resistance movement while the Japanese were here, and I helped him in many small ways. We were so relieved when the Japanese finally left us, and so happy when the British granted us independence. I remember the transfer ceremonies when the Union Jack came down for the last time and our new flag went up.

"We expected so much from independence," he added, "and many of us have been disappointed. Ruling ourselves is much tougher than we realized, but we would never admit it publicly even now. We have made lots of mistakes in this country, most of them quite natural, I guess. I do not think we considered thoroughly enough the policies we adopted, the kind of government we set up, or the way we operated it.

"I don't know too much about the other countries of Southeast Asia," the young Burmese concluded, "but I have a feeling it is the same there, too."

Besides Burma, the free countries of Southeast Asia include

sprawling and insular Indonesia (the former Dutch East Indies), the Philippines (another island nation), peninsular Malaya, and mainland Thailand, Cambodia, Laos, and Vietnam (now split into a Communist state and a non-Communist one). The total land area of the nations of Southeast Asia exceeds 1.6 million square miles.* All these countries, except Thailand (though it did lose some of its territory to both France and Britain), are former colonies of Western nations. The old imperial bonds were severed, however, between 1946 and 1957, and all are independent today, although the independence of Communist North Vietnam is akin to that of the Eastern European satellite countries. Four lesser territories remain under varying forms of Western rule: the island of Singapore (internally self-governing, but Britain retains responsibility for her external affairs); the British possessions of Sarawak, Brunei, and North Borneo on the island of Borneo; Dutch western and Australian eastern New Guinea;† and the Portuguese eastern half of the otherwise Indonesian island of Timor. But it is perhaps only a matter of time before these vestiges of European colonialism will disappear from the southeastern corner of the great Asian land mass.

The contemporary significance of Southeast Asia lies partly in its location. Besides linking the Indian and Pacific Oceans, the two-pronged tropical mainland peninsula and the far-flung string of equatorial islands are situated between a resurgent China under Communist rule and democratically oriented and socialistically inclined India. High mountains separate Southeast Asia from both China and India, except in the northeastern corner, where there is no natural boundary between China and North Vietnam. However, the seas to the east, south, and west, which make Southeast Asia accessible to the world beyond, also form a

---

* The area (in square miles) and population, respectively, of the states of Southeast Asia are as follows: Indonesia (575,450 square miles; 90 million people), Burma (261,610; 20 million), Thailand (200,148; 23 million), the Philippines (115,600; 24 million), Cambodia (66,590; 5 million), South Vietnam (65,000; 12 million), North Vietnam (62,000; 13 million), Laos (88,780; 2 million), and Malaya (50,690; 6.75 million).

† Australia governs northeastern New Guinea as a United Nations trust territory and the southeastern part of the island as its own territorial possession.

boundary that ties this area to the destinies of the vast Asian continent.

The countries of Southeast Asia have recently taken part in the world-wide revolt against European domination—as have India and China—and, with political freedom now attained, cannot help being influenced in this new era by what their neighbors do. The natural resources of the region may directly affect the policies of these giant neighbors toward Southeast Asia, which supplies two-thirds of all the rice entering world trade, produces nearly nine-tenths of the world's natural rubber and half of its tin, and is an important source of coconut products, palm oil, and tungsten, as well as quinine, kapok, and chromium.

Southeast Asia, moreover, has traditionally been a meeting ground of cultures, as evidenced by its diversity of religions, and of conflicting political and economic interests. Today is not basically different from yesterday in this respect, and there is no reason to expect a different kind of tomorrow. In the Far East today, only the nations of Southeast Asia (with the exception of North Vietnam), along with Japan, Formosa, and South Korea— representing a minority of the people and the land—remain non-Communist. It is improbable that any of these countries can retreat from the great ideological and political conflict of our age.

The overwhelming majority of the nearly 200 million people who inhabit the several lands of Southeast Asia are Mongoloid. The ancestors of most of them migrated southward from China many centuries ago. Of today's major population groups, the first to move into the area were the Malays (or Indonesians, as they may be called ethnically), who arrived between 2500 and 1500 B.C. The Malays are found today mainly in Indonesia and the Philippines—where they constitute an overwhelming majority of the inhabitants—and in Malaya, where they are still the single most important ethnic group. The various languages spoken by the Malays are related in character.

The inhabitants of the mainland Southeast Asian countries— Burma, Thailand, Cambodia, Laos, and North and South Vietnam—differ from one another much more than do the peoples of the Philippines or Indonesia. Not only do they constitute distinct ethnic groups, but they also speak quite different languages, and their cultures display greater variation. The Burmese, related to the Tibetans, moved into what is now Burma as early as the ninth century; the Thai, from the kingdom of Nan-Chao in south China, were not widely settled in Southeast Asia until the thirteenth century. The neighboring Lao speak essentially the same language as the Thai and share the same ethnic background. The Cambodians can trace their Southeast Asian ancestry much further back than the Burmese, Thai, or Lao; they are the descendants of the Khmers, whose kingdom became a major state of the Indochinese Peninsula in the ninth century and registered great cultural achievements between then and the end of the twelfth century. The Vietnamese, who live along the coast of the extreme southeastern corner of Asia, came from the Canton area of China; they were conquered by the Chinese before the birth of Christ and remained under their rule for a thousand years.

Yet, despite their differences, the independent lands of both insular and mainland Southeast Asia share many characteristics. All except Thailand are former Western colonies that have regained their freedom since 1946, and all are underdeveloped economically. Malaya and the Philippines probably have the most advanced economies, and Laos the least. The products of the various national economies are essentially the same, although some countries (like Malaya) specialize in rubber and tin, and others (like Burma) in rice. These economies, which are agricultural and extractive, depend heavily on shifts in international prices, since a large share of the area's products are shipped abroad. Industrialization is only now beginning, in such lands as Malaya and Thailand, and has not really started at all in others like Cambodia or Laos. Some of the areas of Southeast Asia—the Indonesian island of Java, North Vietnam, and Singapore, in particular—are confronted with serious problems resulting from rapid population growth, while others, such as Burma and Thailand, are underpopulated.

Politically, all the Southeast Asian peoples, except the Thai, are inexperienced in governing themselves. However, this is much less true of the Filipinos, who were deliberately introduced to self-government by the United States, than of the Cambodians or Lao, who were not so assisted by the French. The contemporary political structures everywhere follow the general Western pattern, even in Thailand, and national frontiers follow the boundaries of the old colonial holdings, except for the territories that formerly comprised French Indochina. Today, general political instability characterizes most of these lands, and they all have internal Communist problems of varying seriousness, as well as unsolved minority difficulties. In most of the countries, too, there is disappointment with the results of independence and with democratically oriented institutions; and almost everywhere, the army has attained political importance. All these nations, except Thailand, are new at the task of making and executing foreign policy, but old in the habit of being suspicious of the formerly colonial West. Their foreign policies differ frequently as to means, but far less in terms of objectives.

### Pre-European Political Heritage

Before the era of European colonialism, Southeast Asia was strongly influenced by India.* This heritage is still an important aspect of contemporary life in the area, although it is more evident socially and culturally than politically and economically. Even politically, however, the legacy of the pre-Western era lingers on, despite its modification during the period of European colonialism. Some of the states of present-day Southeast Asia were states before the coming of the Westerner—lacking all the trappings of the modern state, but states nevertheless. As many Burmese still delight in reminding Englishmen, there was a unified Burmese kingdom by 1044, several decades before William the Conqueror crossed the English Channel. The existence of a pre-Western Burma served as a stimulus to Burmese nationalism as it evolved in the British period, and today it gives this nationalism depth and strength.

There were also regional, loosely structured commercial empires in pre-Western Indonesia: Srivijaya, which was based in

---

* The traditional culture of Southeast Asia is well treated by Lucian W. Pye in his chapter on the area (pp. 69-81) in Gabriel A. Almond and James S. Coleman, *The Politics of Developing Areas* (Princeton, N.J.: Princeton University Press, 1960).

Sumatra and appeared as a major trading power in the seventh century; Sailendra, which started in central Java, emerged as a kingdom in the eighth century and subsequently merged with Srivijaya; and Majapahit, which was based in east Java and lasted from the late thirteenth century to the early sixteenth. The influence of these empires extended not only throughout most of the Indonesian Archipelago but also up the Malay Peninsula into lower Thailand and apparently beyond. None of them, however, ever ruled politically over all of Indonesia.

There was no united Indonesian state when the Dutch came. They created the national political entity of Indonesia as it is known today, just as the Spanish unified the Philippines and the British Malaya. Indonesian nationalists, nonetheless, regard their country as the descendant of Srivijaya and Majapahit. The knowledge, however imperfect, of these ancient states gives Indonesians a sense of their own history, and their pride in this has aided the development of a national consciousness that has considerable political relevance today.

All the countries of Southeast Asia were absolute monarchies before the Western period. Although the various kings, emperors, and sultans generally had advisory councils to assist them, these represented the court elite and cannot be considered sources from which national legislatures might have emerged. There was some popular participation in government on the local level, but the degree varied from country to country, and its importance is exaggerated by nationalist writers. Government from the center of authority in pre-Western times was highly personal, arbitrary, and much feared by the populace. The elite ruled the peasantry with an iron hand, the peasants could not register effective objection, and the two classes existed, for the most part, in quite separate worlds, politically and otherwise.

Throughout the period of European colonial domination, the same general relationship between the rulers and the ruled continued, with only limited modification, in most of the Southeast Asian countries. Unfortunately, the situation today is basically similar. Thai Prime Minister Sarit Thanarat, Indonesian President Sukarno, and South Vietnamese President Ngo Dinh Diem would have been at home as imperial governors or pre-imperial monarchs. The tradition of absolutism dies slowly.

Much of the court structure and many of the devices of government in the pre-Western period were Hindu-derived, in spite of the advent of Islam in the fifteenth century. The Southeast Asian states borrowed heavily from India's governmental structure, legal procedure, and political philosophy. Although this borrowing was sufficiently extensive to justify calling these countries "Hinduized," it nowhere led to the creation of truly unified political units. India's influence in political matters is further evidenced by the blending of the religious and political identity of the ruler in Burma, Thailand, Cambodia, and Laos, as well as in Moslem Indonesia and Malaya. U Nu, Burma's present-day political and religious messiah, is much more comprehensible as a traditional ruler than as a Western-style prime minister.

Government in most of the pre-colonial states of Southeast Asia was much less formidable institutionally than in pre-Renaissance Europe. Rules were made and enforced, and differences among the elite were reconciled, but effective centralized authority was the exception rather than the rule. Most regimes were notoriously unstable; revolt and murder were often the essence of the political process. The absence of a popular base to pre-Western government and the continual jockeying for power among the few participants in politics encouraged this weakness and instability. The desire to govern also varied from ruler to ruler, and the effect of this variation was maximized by the comparatively limited administrative structure that supported the state.

The country in Southeast Asia least influenced by India was Vietnam, the colonial ward of giant China for a thousand years and, recently, again the objective of Chinese imperialism. One of the main results of this long association was the development of a Vietnamese mandarin bureaucracy on the Chinese model. China's political impact upon Southeast Asia otherwise was surprisingly slight, even though the Chinese were foreign suzerains to several countries farther south from time to time.

**The Western Impact**

The form and much of the substance of government and politics in today's Southeast Asia bear the strong imprint of Western colonialism. This imprint varies according to differences in the nature of the country colonized and of the colonizing power, and according to periodic changes in the objectives of colonization.

The West began the wholesale colonization of Southeast Asia in the sixteenth century. First came the Portuguese and the Spanish, then the Dutch, who were later joined by the English and the French, and finally by the Americans. Britain colonized Burma, Malaya, Singapore, and North Borneo; the Netherlands controlled Indonesia; and France governed Vietnam, Cambodia, and Laos (which it lumped together artificially as Indochina). Spain and later the United States governed the Philippines; each left quite a distinct legacy for the Filipino people. Thailand never became a Western colony, but was strongly influenced by the Europeans politically, as well as economically and culturally.

As for the objectives of the colonial powers, the Dutch were mainly interested in economic control, while the Spanish also sought to convert the heathen. Spain indeed succeeded in converting the Filipinos; more than 92 per cent of them are today Christians. This contrasts vividly with the continued Buddhist orientation of the Burmese, Thai, Cambodians, and Lao; the predominance of Islam in Indonesia and Malaya; and the retention by a majority of the Vietnamese people of their traditional Chinese-derived spiritual mixture of Confucianism, Buddhism, Taoism, and ancestor worship.

The French cultural legacy in Vietnam is impressive; France placed great emphasis on colonial expansion for purposes of national prestige as well as economic aggrandizement. The British, like the Dutch, were economically motivated, but unlike any of the other European metropolitan states, they recognized comparatively early the inevitability of self-government, if not of independence. The United States, which spilled over into the western Pacific in the enthusiasm of its initial years as a world power, sought to prepare the Philippines for ultimate political emancipation; but this policy reflected recognition of the advanced state of Filipino nationalism at the time of the American takeover as much as it did American liberalism.

The full burden of colonialism was assumed reluctantly at first by some of the European powers, which initially did not want to bear the responsibilities of government. Indeed, colonial objectives were pursued with only limited enthusiasm by most of the home governments during much of the period of Western imperial expansion. Partly for this reason, life in the Southeast Asian territories, especially for the masses, was little affected by the foreign intruders until the twentieth century, by which time colonial governmental responsibility had not only been established, but was being willingly enlarged to protect investments in the developing economies.*

The most important aspect of the European impact upon Southeast Asia was the stimulus the Western presence gave to a social and economic life that for centuries had remained static. The old economic objective of self-subsistence was supplemented, to an ever-increasing extent, by the new goal of export for overseas markets, while the former dominant identification with the village or the tribe was steadily displaced, as the Western penetration proceeded, by the new loyalty of nationalism. The overwhelming majority of the people of Southeast Asia are still subsistence farmers, but the fate of their nations depends largely on the export of various agricultural and mineral products.

Before the coming of the West, a sense of the community was the outstanding characteristic of the Southeast Asian's outlook. The West, however, introduced a sense of individualism, as well as a nationalistic pride. A revolution in values was, and is still being, accomplished. The disparity between the new collective loyalty of nationalism and the liberal individualism brought in by the West may explain some of the frustration so evident in Southeast Asia today.

The Western presence was felt ultimately in all phases of Southeast Asian life, although the extent of the impact on some traditional ways probably cannot yet be fully judged. The general context of living was changed by the European rulers: Local

---

* Prior to the twentieth century, the imperial powers were primarily interested in trade in native products.

wars were ended, economic life was reorganized, and new medical techniques helped to produce, among other results, major population increases. In the mid-nineteenth century, there were probably no more than 10 million people in all Southeast Asia; today, there are nine times that many in Indonesia alone. The period of Western dominance in Southeast Asia was an unparalleled age of stability and opportunity, as is evidenced by the large-scale migration of Chinese and Indians to the region.

For the most part, the changes introduced by the Europeans were not designed for the welfare of the indigenous populations. But the native governments displaced by the foreigners had not been notable for their concern for the welfare of their people either. The main objectives of colonialism (and they met with varying degrees of fulfillment) were profits from the operation of the overseas possessions, political power, and prestige. Yet, there is no question that the local inhabitants benefited from many of the economic, educational, and health measures introduced by the ruling powers, whatever their motivation. Moreover, the liberalism of the British and even of the French and the Dutch, as it was evolving in Europe, could not help reverberating in their overseas territories.

The ideas of democracy and parliamentary (or representative) government were among the contributions of the West to Southeast Asia. The Philippines, following half a century of American rule, modeled its independent government after that of the United States, while the Burmese and Malayans patterned theirs after the British example. The general structure of the state, moreover, democratic or not, is a legacy of the European imperial association. Indonesia, ruled by a multiplicity of princes and chieftains before colonization, adopted a national political structure as a result of its experience under Dutch rule. The Thai state remains monarchal in form, as it was before the Western era, but the revolution of 1932 made it a constitutional monarchy and introduced other political devices of European origin, continuing a process that had been begun earlier by the great monarch Chulalongkorn. Not only prime ministers, presidents, cabinets, legislatures, and constitutions, but also various other paraphernalia of modern government, such as planning commissions and regulatory agencies, have been adopted by the Southeast Asian lands.

In addition to democracy and nationalism, the West gave Southeast Asia its other most prominent contemporary political and economic ideologies—socialism and Communism. The socialism of Burma is a mixture of influences emanating from Britain, continental Europe, and Russia, with heavy post-independence borrowing from Israel and Yugoslavia. The Communism of Vietnam's Ho Chi-minh, as it emerged during the years of struggle against the French, was derived from Marx, Lenin, and Stalin. Internationalism, in its twentieth-century meaning—the interdependence of many countries—is another European contribution. Trade relations between Southeast Asia and other regions have existed since ancient times, and the area has long been subject to a multitude of foreign cultural influences, but political relations with countries outside the region were comparatively limited before the coming of the West. Political parties, labor unions, newspapers and radio stations, and many other elements of the total modern political process also are Western in origin. But the inexperience of the Southeast Asian countries in self-government and the very fact that they remained isolated from other nations during the years of colonial domination can also be attributed to the West.

### Nationalism

The nationalist movements that have so completely changed the political face of Southeast Asia were a direct reaction to foreign domination and the disruption of the traditional way of life. They were, and are, the core of the complicated process of adjustment.

The Western imperial rulers stimulated the development of nationalism in a variety of ways—not the least of which were their very presence and rule. The centralized governments they established, together with the revolutionary changes they effected in transportation and communications, drew the peoples of each of the Southeast Asian lands closer together and altered the way in which they regarded both themselves and outsiders. Development by the colonial powers of national economies—based on the export of rice, rubber, tin, and other products—had a centralizing effect that further encouraged nationalism's evolution. Nationalism as an idea, moreover, had behind it more than a century's development in Europe, where the achievements of the seemingly mighty colonial powers were partially explained in terms of national solidarity.

The colonial authority was the common foe and, as such, cemented together an otherwise frequently diverse collection of aroused elements. The imperial power had taken away independence, which meant that Burmese and Indonesians, for example, were inferior to Englishmen and Dutchmen—a status that ever-larger numbers of Burmese and Indonesians were unwilling to accept.

The motivation of the first nationalists and those of succeeding generations differed little. Both sought to counteract the impact of Western dominance and put together a new social structure with the remains of their heritage and the contributions of the foreigner. The immediate objectives of the first and subsequent nationalists, however, were not the same. Initially, nationalism in most of the Southeast Asian lands was basically apolitical in character, seeking only to revitalize and modernize aspects of the indigenous culture. As resentment of foreign rule grew, however, the nature and aims of the nationalist movements changed, and nationalism acquired the political goal of self-government, which in turn was quickly transformed into the objective of independence. Nevertheless, nationalism remained, and is still today, a multisided phenomenon, embracing the economic, social, religious, and artistic—as well as the political—life of the Southeast Asian countries. Now that independence has been attained, it still seeks to create national societies in the wake of the disruptions of alien rule.

Even in the years of bitter struggle against imperial control, nationalism in Southeast Asia was more than antiforeignism (although it was unquestionably that, too). From the start, it sought to link people sharing certain characteristics, however ill-defined at any moment, in a union of common consciousness akin to the manner in which Britons, Frenchmen, and Americans regarded themselves as distinct divisions of humanity. Two goals essentially were, and still are, sought: freedom in all respects from external control, and revival and utilization of the worth while in the national heritage. In the first half of this century, the aim was to oust the foreigner in order to replace him and his domination with a new era of national achievement and prosperity. In pursuit of this, the nationalists tried to use the tools of their conquerors—their machines, their science, their ideologies, and, above all, their governing and integrative institution of the national state.

That nationalism should have emerged as a significant force first in the Philippines is not surprising. The Spanish presence in those islands dated back to the sixteenth century; and Spain, in fact, unified the Filipino people for the first time through the single political administration she established and the common religion of Christianity. Nationalism expressed itself in the Philippines in a variety of ways by the mid-nineteenth century, including hundreds of minor revolts and a major one in 1872. The Filipinos were engaged in a full-scale revolutionary effort to oust the Spanish at the time of the American acquisition of the colony at the end of the century.

In the other Southeast Asian lands, nationalism has been largely a development of the twentieth century. Indonesian nationalism first took the form of the essentially cultural Budi Utomo, founded in 1908. Shortly thereafter Sarekat Islam, Indonesia's first mass nationalist body, was founded. The Young Men's Buddhist Association, formed in 1906, was Burma's first institutional nationalist reaction to British rule, and it, too, was succeeded by a more political body, the General Council of Burmese Associations. Comparable developments took place in Vietnam, but nationalism in Malaya, Cambodia, and Laos was mainly a product of the years after World War II. A paternalistic British colonial policy and the existence of large and separate communities of Malays and Chinese, who had migrated to Malaya largely during the British period, were the main factors hindering the earlier development of Malayan nationalism. Cambodia and Laos were sufficiently isolated—and kept so by France—that it took the era of Japanese rule during World War II to bring into being nationalist movements in these two lands. Thai nationalism, which could hardly seek political freedom from a nonexistent alien ruler, found its first expression instead in various moves to eliminate the economic dominance of its large Chinese minority.

Although the rate of development and even the substance of the several nationalist movements varied, there were also similarities, such as their predominantly cultural rather than political nature at first. Moreover, the initial nationalist movements were generally characterized by a distinct democratic orientation—partly because both democracy and nationalism have their roots in the desire of peoples to govern themselves, and partly because the colonial powers whom the nationalists sought to displace, and imitate, were democracies. A major exception were the Communists, who usually regard the ouster of the foreigner as merely a step toward their ultimate revolutionary goal. Most of Burma's young nationalists of the 1930's were intellectually sympathetic to Communism, and Communists were important in the development of Vietnamese and Indonesian nationalism.

In all the Southeast Asian lands, the nationalist movement had its origins among the comparatively Westernized elite, who were the most uprooted element of the colonial society and the one most aware of the differences between the foreign way of doing things and traditional habits. The imperial ruler was not the only object of their resentment; there was strong nationalist sentiment against the non-Western minorities in all these countries. Indonesia's Sarekat Islam was anti-Chinese rather than anti-Dutch in its first years, and the anti-Indian and anti-Chinese riots in Burma in the 1930's offered sharp contrast to the absence of comparable violence against British nationals.

But the two most significant similarities among the various nationalist movements in terms of consequences—both past and potential—are probably their mass character and their role in encouraging social and economic change beyond immediate political requirements. There are still countless inhabitants of the lands of Southeast Asia who remain comparatively untouched by this great force of their times, but the twentieth century has clearly been characterized by a growing mass national self-awareness, as well as the establishment of a more direct bond between people and state than ever before in the history of the area. Popular enthusiasm is not as evident, however, for the less exciting task of weaving the social, economic, and political fabric of the new national structures.

Early nationalism also had a distinct economic orientation, which it has retained. The nationalist leaders proclaimed that colonialism was a main cause of their low living standards, and they promised a better material existence once the foreign ruler had been driven out. As a means toward this end, the nationalists —or most of them—vigorously endorsed large-scale state participation in the economy. Some were Communists, more were socialists, few were capitalists. The imperial power was itself capitalist, which colored their economic thinking considerably—particularly since it was largely the shortcomings of capitalism that had occasioned the injustice of overseas colonies in the first place (or so the nationalists had read in their Marxist books). A major goal of nationalism throughout the region has always been the ending of foreign economic—and political—control as part of the process of redevelopment of the national economy for the welfare of the general citizenry, with the state itself as the main means to this end.

Today, nationalism in Southeast Asia poses several problems, probably the most important one being: Can popular support be developed for the positive purpose of nation-building, or does mass nationalism require the stimulation of a common foreign foe? The answer could be crucial to the future evolution of the countries of this part of the world.

### The Coming of Independence

On the eve of World War II, there were few who expected that nationalism in Southeast Asia would achieve its primary goal of immediate political independence in the near future. The nationalist movements were increasing in strength, but the colonial regimes still seemed strong. The only country with expectations of early independence was the Philippines, to which the United

States had promised emancipation by 1944 (somewhat to the annoyance of the other colonial powers). But the war changed everything. The old imperial regimes were toppled, and the Western colonial rulers were revealed as something less than invincible. The Japanese gave the countries they conquered some of the trappings of independence, and thereby whetted appetites. The colonial powers were never able to restore their imperial regimes to the prewar status quo.

The Philippines was the first to obtain its independence; the transfer of authority took place on July 4, 1946. Burma came next—on January 4, 1948, at 3:40 A.M., an hour deemed auspicious by the astrologers. The transition to independence in these countries was comparatively easy and unmarked by bloodshed. This was not the case, however, with the Netherlands' Indonesian and France's Indochinese possessions. The Indonesians fought a four-year anticolonial war to earn their freedom, and the nationalists and Communists struggled in French Indochina for eight years. Real independence for Cambodia and Laos can be dated from the end of that war in 1954, which also resulted in the division of Vietnam into separate Communist and non-Communist states. Malaya became free in 1957, partially as a result of Britain's planned nation-building efforts.

Before independence, opposition to foreign control gave unity of direction to the nationalist cause and generated mass support. The response to the hard work of self-government and economic self-support, however, has been less enthusiastic, although Burma's leaders in particular have tried to stimulate popular backing for their policies with their heavily propagandized *Pyidawtha* (Happy Land) economic and social-welfare programs.

Throughout the area (with the exception of Indonesia), nationalism since independence has lost some of its antiforeign character. (It will never lose all of it.) Simultaneously, it seems to have become more positive; there is at least some enthusiasm for the task of building nations as functioning entities now that political freedom has been achieved. This enthusiasm is limited, however, to a comparatively small sector of the populace, and one that does not seem to increase appreciably.

Nationalism has changed, as have its leaders and followers.

It is probably less important today than it was on the eve of independence or immediately afterwards. Nevertheless, it remains the single most important political force in Southeast Asia. And foreign intervention could quickly arouse it to positive action. Whether anything else can do so remains to be seen.

Foremost among the reasons for reduced mass nationalist enthusiasm is the widespread dissatisfaction with the record of the national governments in several of the newly independent countries. The quick improvements forecast by the nationalist leaders in the years of struggle against the colonial governments simply have not been forthcoming. The masses were promised higher living standards with the departure of the Europeans, and, on the whole, they have been disappointed. The average man remains poor by Western (if not Asian) standards, but, more important, he remains poor by the standards of his stimulated expectations.

The standard of living has visibly improved in Thailand in recent years, but Thailand was not a colony. It is even higher in Malaya, but economic discontent was not a major stimulus in Malayan nationalism. Widespread disappointment does exist in Indonesia, where living costs have spiraled in the post-independence years; educated and uneducated alike have serious difficulties in making ends meet. The Indonesian population, meanwhile, continues to increase rapidly, and the economic pie is being cut into ever-smaller pieces.

Mass discontent is limited in Burma, but there is major dissatisfaction among the educated and professional classes, including the army. Burmese socialism in the first decade after independence was a bumbling kind of socialism; independence, accordingly, did not prove to be what had been expected. In Cambodia, where nationalism developed rapidly and there was no long period of mounting anticipation, there is correspondingly less disappointment. In both the Philippines and Laos, on the other hand, there has been dissatisfaction because past conservative governments in these countries have failed to address themselves to the problems of the rural peasantry. Large-scale American financial assistance to anti-Communist South Vietnam probably has effectively prevented the development of serious economic discontent in that land, but there is resentment engendered by the limited political freedom permitted by President Ngo Dinh Diem, who has tightened control over the country in view of the continuing subversive threat posed by the adjacent Communist state. North Vietnam has not been without its difficulties either; there has been at least one serious uprising stemming from discontent with the regime's agrarian reforms.

The most important reason for the widespread dissatisfaction with the record of the new nationalist governments is unquestionably the failure of these governments to find solutions for pressing problems. But this is not the only reason. Nationalism has lost some of its old fire in Southeast Asia; it no longer has its onetime "do-or-die" quality. Anti-Dutch nationalists in Indonesia, for example, could recover from setbacks at the hands of the ruling colonialists, but it is more difficult, psychologically, to recover from setbacks brought on by problems that seem to defy solution. The enthusiasm of the Indonesians during the great anticolonial struggle of the late 1940's against the Dutch has been dissipated; no longer is there the same dedication, the *esprit de corps*, or the confidence.

In addition, nationalism today has serious rivals for the allegiance of masses and elite alike—Communism and separatism. In terms of organizational strength and potential votes in a free election, Indonesia's Communist Party is probably the single most important avowedly political organization in that country today; it is also the second largest Communist party in all Asia. In Laos also, the Communists are strong. They have competed in the past for power and popular support through the Pathet Lao rebels, based largely in the part of the country bordering North Vietnam, and through the Laotian Patriotic Front, which was much stronger, particularly in the countryside, than was indicated by its abysmal showing in the rigged elections of April, 1960. Although Communist insurrectionists have been routed by the army in Burma, the country's leaders agree that Communism as an ideological force remains a serious threat; it continues to attract many politically inclined students at influential Rangoon University.

In Indonesia, Laos, and Burma—as elsewhere in Southeast Asia—the Communists preach that the leaders of the post-independence governments have failed to fulfill their promises. They have failed, say the Communists, because something more than an independent national state structure is necessary. The state must be organized in a particular way—the Communist way. The Communists' claim that they can do more for the people finds ready support among many of those disappointed with the record of independence (as in Indonesia). Others, disillusioned once, tend to look with suspicion upon the promises of another new wave of political hucksters. Still others recognize Communism as a threat to various things they cherish and do not listen at all. But enough listen, and believe, to make Communism a real rival to nationalism for the loyalty of some of the peoples of Southeast Asia today.

The other rival of nationalism, separatism—"little nationalism," it might be called—is divisive nationalism carried to the extreme. Before independence, various peoples joined together to fight for freedom, but they had very little in common; still others found themselves linked after independence, which not all of them had wanted. Although Javanese and Sumatrans fought side by side in Indonesia's colonial war against the Dutch, differences do exist between the peoples of these two important islands and among the peoples who populate each of them. The Sumatran rebellion of 1958, which had its roots in both political and economic problems, demonstrated in many ways the mythical aspect of Indonesian nationalism. This is not to say that there is no such thing as Indonesian nationalism—simply that it is not what Indonesia's leaders say it is. It is less broadly based, it is felt with varying degrees of intensity, and it is apparently not strong enough to prevent the outbreak of such separatist rebellions as have occurred in Sulawesi (Celebes), Malukus (Moluccas), and Sumatra. Strong regional feelings exist elsewhere in the Indonesian islands, but they have not flared into rebellion against the government for various reasons.

The situation is somewhat similar in Burma, which also has separatist problems. The Burmans, the largest of the several ethnic groups that comprise the Burmese people as a national entity, were the leaders in the fight for independence from British rule. Some of the minorities even feared independence, with the expectation that they might be treated less well by the Burmans than they had been by the British. The most important continuing rebellion in Burma today is led not by the Communists but by a faction of the partly Christianized Karens, who constitute one of the more important indigenous racial minorities in the country. Rebellion exists, too, in the Shan states, bordering Thailand, where the inhabitants are more like the Thai than the Burmans. In addition, the Arakanese in western Burma want a separate state of their own within the semifederal Union of Burma, as does another minority, the Mons, a few of whom also are still in revolt against the central government.

Indonesia and Burma are not the only countries with unsolved minority problems, but they are among the lands where the forces of separatism, opposed to the current national system, have proved most persistent. Although there is no evidence that nationalism is on the defensive, separatist tendencies have seriously challenged it, leaving these nations weaker as political units. The divisions afflicting Vietnam and Laos cannot really be said to be rooted in separatism, but are the result of the efforts of the Communists, who in these two lands at least have exploited nationalist sentiment more than separatist feelings.

During the first decade and a half after World War II, the nationalist leadership sought to lay the governmental foundations for the new states they had brought into being. They also began the task of giving life to the policies of which they had long dreamed. And for the first time in a long while—centuries in the cases of the Filipinos and the Indonesians—Southeast Asians resumed control of their relations with other countries. When the political transition from the European colonial period is completed—as it should be within the next decade in Singapore, North Borneo, New Guinea, and Timor—an era in the post-independence existence of the Southeast Asian countries will have come to an end.

Two

# FIRST CHOICE OF GOVERNMENTS

SOME NATIONS are fortunate in being able to choose the form of government that will rule over them. Indonesia and Burma, to cite two of the newly independent lands of Southeast Asia, had the opportunity to make such a choice in the late 1940's—influenced, of course, by such forces as the general Western democratic impact on the rest of the world and their own peculiar experiences with particular European colonial powers. Both decided to model their governmental institutions on the Western parliamentary democracies, borrowing many features, including political parties. In neither land, however, has democracy worked as well as those who fought for independence thought it would.

The Burmese were so unsuccessful at first that a year after the British had left, the entire country except for the capital city was in the hands of various nondemocratic forces (Communists and other kinds of insurrectionists). Although Burma survived this period of rebellion, by the tenth year of independence the civilian leadership was so divided and the government so ineffective in maintaining law and order that the army had to take over. Yet, Burma's civilian Premier U Nu, who returned to office following the military's voluntary relinquishment of authority after eighteen months of rule, loudly proclaims democracy's worth and relevance to his people—and apparently means it.

Indonesian President Sukarno has a different message. As Burma did, his nation set up a government patterned after the democratic forms of the West. But Indonesia—as in the case of Burma

—also has made only limited progress toward solution of its problems in the years since emancipation from colonial rule and has actually regressed in some key economic fields. These problems, President Sukarno has stated, have not been tackled more effectively principally because Western-style democracy is ill-suited to Indonesia.

The differences between the positions of Nu and Sukarno are especially paradoxical since neither Burma nor Indonesia has done particularly well in governing itself. There are those in Indonesia who think as Nu does, and those in Burma who share Sukarno's outlook.

Of the eight lands in Southeast Asia that have so far gained their freedom from colonial rule in the period since World War II, four seem to have sought initially to establish Western-style democratic governments: the Philippines, Burma, Malaya, and Indonesia. The leaders of Singapore also have espoused the democratic approach and presumably will continue to do so after the island becomes fully independent. The four other newly independent countries of Southeast Asia did not begin their free existence in a democratically oriented manner.

### The Philippines

The Philippines, the first of these countries to gain freedom after World War II, modeled its governmental institutions on those of the United States, which had been its colonial ruler for almost half a century. It became, however, a unitary rather than a federal state.

The constitution, drafted in 1935, provides for the separation of powers into executive, legislative, and judicial branches. During the tutelary Commonwealth period that began in 1934 under President Manuel Quezon, one party actually held power. It was not until after World War II that a two-party system developed in the Islands. But the two parties (Nationalists and Liberals) are even less distinguishable than are the American Democratic and Republican parties.

The Philippine Congress is bicameral, the upper and lower

houses bearing the same names (Senate and House of Representatives) as their American models. The committee organization of the two chambers, their powers (such as that of the Senate in ratifying treaties), and their interrelationship and relative importance also follow the American pattern to a remarkable degree.

The presidency, with constitutional powers much like those of its American namesake, is in fact an even more powerful office in relation to the other branches of government. The Philippine president possesses, for example, "item veto authority" over money and tariff bills, meaning that he can strike out parts of such legislation. His dominant role in the government, the result of political factors as well as the constitutional allocation of authority, is illustrated by the fact that Congress has never been able to pass a bill over his veto. The Supreme Court, although more involved in political questions than its American counterpart, is highly respected and seemingly secure as a key institution of the government, largely because of its independent character.

The national governmental institutions of the Philippine Republic have functioned successfully. The policies of the official leadership since independence may be open to criticism, but it cannot be said of government in the Philippines that it has failed to govern. The state of law and order there is superior to that in other newly independent lands in Southeast Asia, and the government's fiat has a wide area of authority.

Filipino presidents have been able to direct the executive organs of the state in a constitutional manner and to hold the country together. More than any other state in Southeast Asia, the Philippine Republic has achieved a notable record of continuity and performance in its governmental institutions. Congress is an important part of the total decision-making machinery of the state, being neither the rubber stamp of the executive (as Burma's Parliament was for the greater part of the first ten years of independence) nor a device to be discarded at the wish of a dictator (as happened to the legislature of Sukarno's Indonesia in 1960). The Philippine president and Congress have not always agreed, and they have often worked at cross-purposes, but they have been partners, on the whole, in the process of policy determination.

However, democracy is something more than institutions that work formally. Although Filipino democracy has developed institutions capable of effective government, those who control these institutions appear to be remote from the great mass of the country's people. They do not understand their wants or, if they do understand them, do not sympathize with them. What made the late Ramón Magsaysay such an unusual figure in Filipino politics when he was President of the Republic was the fact that he was one of the first leaders to comprehend and sympathize with the problems of the masses. The smashing proportions of his election victory in 1953 made him, moreover, a power in his own right above his party, to which he had only shortly before shifted his allegiance, and he was able to lend a fuller meaning to democratic government in the Philippines than any politician before or since. Unfortunately, the popular President was killed in a plane crash in March, 1957.

Carlos P. García, who moved up to the presidency from the vice presidency after Magsaysay's death, was a politician of the old Filipino school. He was of the conservative, educated elite which serves as the almost exclusive source for Philippine political leadership. He totally lacked Magsaysay's contact with, and sympathy for, the masses, but he knew how to take care of himself on the treacherous low roads of Filipino political in-fighting. Manuel Manahan, a devoted disciple of Magsaysay's, ran as one of three opponents to García in the 1957 elections and garnered 21 per cent of the vote, but his party, the newly formed Progressives, competing for the first time in an election, won no national offices.

Land-tenure conditions and rural living standards in general are regarded by the peasantry as unsatisfactory. For the peasants, there is no real choice between the Nationalists and the Liberals. Both parties survive—indeed, even flourish—by means of the adroit vote-coralling efforts of local representatives, despite the absence of any real popular support for them. The Communist-controlled Hukbalahap* rebellion that reached its peak in 1950 did not enjoy mass support in a true sense. But its appeal to the discontented peasantry in some areas contrasted vividly with the lack of real backing for the two major parties. The man who did more than any other single person to extinguish the insurgents' challenge was Ramón Magsaysay. As Minister of Defense, he gave the rebels land, settled them, and also fought the insurrection. However, even as President, Magsaysay was not able to alleviate the plight of the peasantry overnight.

The problem of Filipino democracy appears to lie not in its structure of government, but in the semioligarchic character of its politicians. Filipino politics also continues to be highly personalized and, as a result, unstable (with leaders and followers alike switching from one major party to the other)—but neither as personalized nor as unstable as most of the other lands of Southeast Asia.

### Burma

Burma, like the Philippines, was ruled by a colonial power that made concessions to nationalist demands before force was used against it. The British responded favorably to the insistence of the Burmese nationalists for a greater voice in their government, ultimately granting them independence in January, 1948.†

As in the cases of other recently colonial countries, the Burmese modeled their government on that of the departing metropolitan power. Burma picked the parliamentary form of democratic government with premier and cabinet responsible to the lower house of a bicameral national legislature. Britain had a premier, and the Burmese had had one in the prewar colonial government,

---

* An abbreviation for the Tagalog words meaning "People's Army against the Japanese." Formed in central Luzon in 1942, the Huks fought vigorously against the Japanese. After the war, they rose in revolt against the newly independent republican government.

† Burma's advance toward independence unquestionably benefited from the fact that the country was ruled until 1937 as part of British India, where Congress-led nationalism was an increasingly momentous force. Burma was more advanced constitutionally than any other Southeast Asian country (except for the Philippines) before 1941.

so the choice was a natural one. In addition, Burma's constitution-makers created a president whose functions were mainly ceremonial. The prime minister, selected from the lower house, chooses the members of his cabinet, and premier and cabinet alike are responsible to the lower chamber. Representation in this house, the 250-member Chamber of Deputies, is based on population.

Although the nationalist revolt against British rule was led largely by the majority Burmans, there are other peoples indigenous to the country whose acquiesence was necessary to launch independent Burma as a state; the Shans, Karens, Kachins, and Chins are the most important of these. The Union of Burma, accordingly, was established as a quasi-federal state. Burma proper—the heart of the country, including within its expanse most of the inhabitants, many major cities, and the richest agricultural land—is ruled directly by the central government in Rangoon just as if it were a unitary state. In addition, five states —the Shan, Karen, Kachin, Chin, and Kayah states—exist as partly autonomous units of the Burmese Union. The powers granted to them by the constitution are limited, however, and the states are dependent on the national government for sufficient revenue.

Besides taking cognizance of the diversity of its population through this quasi-federal arrangement, the fathers of Burma's constitution also provided for a second house, a 125-member Chamber of Nationalities. The semiautonomous states and Burma proper possess constitutionally set representation in this body—not unlike the static numerical representation of each state in the American Senate, although the constituent units of the Union of Burma are not equally represented in the Chamber of Nationalities. Like Britain's House of Lords, Burma's second chamber has only nominal authority.

The elections of April, 1947, for the Constituent Assembly that drew up Burma's constitution produced an overwhelming majority for the nationalist body that had won independence, the Anti-Fascist People's Freedom League (AFPFL). The Assembly was carried over into the independent period as a legislature, because the scheduled voting for the new parliament established by the constitution had to be postponed as a result of the several insurrections that had broken out at the end of colonial rule. Parliamentary elections were not held for the first time until 1951-52. They were held again, on schedule, in 1956 and, following eighteen months of military rule, in 1960. Various types of corruption marked all these elections, but probably not to the extent that serious injustice resulted in terms of the relative strength of the several political parties in the legislature. The AFPFL won handsome majorities in the first two elections, and U Nu's "clean" faction of the party, which had split in 1958 largely as a result of personal rivalries, did the same in 1960. Each of Burma's three post-independence elections, accordingly, produced one-sided results and no really significant opposition in the Parliament.

This had two important results for the operation of government in Burma: It tended to make the victorious politicians arrogant and even irresponsible at times; and, because there was no effective opposition, it reduced the importance of the Chamber of Deputies in the total decision-making process of Burmese politics. Normally, the legislature is not the decisive organ in the policy-making process if the prime minister enjoys a working majority, but the majority has been so consistently large in Burma that Parliament has not even been a place of debate or effective questioning of the government.

In September-October, 1958, the army took over from Prime Minister U Nu in what was a *coup d'état* in all but name. However, the military subsequently bowed out gracefully. The caretaker administration of Premier General Ne Win permitted the Parliament to continue to sit and consulted it as much as the AFPFL had done. It also held elections to determine its civilian successor. The best evidence of the free character of the voting was the fact that U Nu, whom the army did not want to win, emerged the victor. Nu resumed office in April, 1960.

That it was necessary to have an army government in Burma (and it probably was) is testimony to the ineffective manner in which the politicians had directed the country's government and, perhaps, to the people's degree of readiness for democracy. The "clean" AFPFL government of Premier Nu had been unable even to maintain law and order in the country in September, 1958.

Government in Burma has not been less democratic than in the Philippines, but it has been less effective in governing. Largely for this reason, democratic government is on trial today in Burma more than it is in the Philippines. The reasons behind the better performance of the Philippines include greater experience in self-government under the Americans, a better-trained bureaucracy, the more highly educated character of much of its leadership, and the less severe internal problems it has had to face.

### Malaya

Good government, in the Philippine sense of government that is well run and gets things done, is also found in Malaya, the newest of Southeast Asia's independent lands. A few of the Communist insurrectionists who began their revolt against the state in 1948 hide out in the jungle on both sides of the Thailand border, but security conditions are generally better than in most lands of Southeast Asia. Moreover, Malaya has forged ahead in economic development much more rapidly than any of the other nations.

Malaya's government, headed by Prime Minister Tengku Abdul Rahman, has enjoyed a better than two-thirds majority in the House of Representatives since the 1959 elections, and the ruling Alliance Party has provided, temporarily at least, a political meeting ground for the Malay, Chinese, and Indian communities. Rich in rubber and tin, Malaya has the second highest per-capita income in all Asia (British-governed Brunei on the island of Borneo is highest). Malaya seems to have a very bright future, except for one important consideration: the problem of drawing its diverse races together into a truly viable national society.

The Malays, who are of the same general ethnic stock as the majority of the inhabitants of Indonesia and the Philippines, are the indigenous people (at least in modern times) of Malaya. Before the British came, there were Chinese in what is now Malaya, but the great influx began after British rule had brought prosperity and security. Many of the Chinese came to make their fortunes and go back to China; some returned, but far more did not. The men who remained were joined subsequently by Chinese women and formed a community apart from the Moslem Malays, who strongly disliked such habits of the infidel newcomers as pork-eating. The Chinese, in turn, displayed an unmistakable air of superiority toward the Malays, whom they regarded as an inferior people. The British, for their part, compounded difficulties in the long run by following a paternalistic policy toward the less advanced Malays that failed to prepare them for competitive living with the aggressive Chinese.

Today, out of a population of almost 7 million, half are Malaysian (Malays and Indonesians), 37 per cent Chinese, 11 per cent Indian and Pakistani, and 2 per cent Eurasian and European. The Malays, then, are the single most important ethnic group in the country. The Chinese, however, are just as prolific as the Malays and have fewer deaths among their children, so their percentage of the population may be expected to increase.

The principal importance of the Chinese lies not in their numbers, but in their domination of major sectors of the nation's economy; the Malays have shown no particular interest in, or talent for, commercial activity. Yet, the economic predominance of the Chinese is not reflected in either the pro-Malay policies of the Alliance government or the constitutionally protected "special position" of the Malays (engaged primarily in rice farming, teaching, the police, and government service).

Despite the favoritism shown the less-developed Malays, the government is basically democratic. It was modeled on the parliamentary system of Britain, but unlike Britain, Malaya is a federal state. The two houses of the national legislature are possessed of real authority, although money bills may originate only in the lower house. The Senate, the upper house, is filled partly by appointment and partly by indirect election. It can hold off for one year legislation desired by the other chamber, and without its consent (by a two-thirds vote), no constitutional amendment can be adopted. The other chamber, the House of Representatives, is more powerful, since it is the body from which the prime minister is chosen and to which he and the cabinet are responsible, although members of either house may serve in other

43861

ministerial posts. The prime minister is selected by the paramount ruler (*Yang di-Pertuan Agong*), but this is only a matter of form when one party enjoys as large a majority as the Alliance does today. The paramount ruler himself is "elected" for a five-year term from among themselves by the Malay rulers of nine of the eleven states that make up federal Malaya. These states are descendants of the independent states that preceded British rule. Their rulers must be consulted on any change in policy affecting Malay privileges.

Several political parties exist in Malaya, but only one of these has shown itself to be strong at the polls nationally: the Alliance, which is at the same time a party and *not* a party. Basically an electoral coalition, it includes the United Malays National Organization (UMNO), the Malayan Chinese Association (MCA), and the Malayan Indian Congress (MIC), all of which retain their separate organizational identities. There is dissatisfaction within both the Malay and Chinese communities over the approaches of the UMNO and the MCA to relations with the other communities. The moderate pro-Alliance leadership of the UMNO finds itself challenged in many Malay constituencies by the followers of the conservative, Marxist-inclined, anti-Chinese Pan Malayan Islamic Party. During the 1959 election campaign, the MCA split over the question of continued cooperation within the Alliance framework, and an influential faction bolted the coalition. The Alliance now possesses a more than two-thirds majority in the House of Representatives, but the possibility of a split before the next elections, in 1964 or earlier,* cannot be discounted since even the MCA group that stayed with the party in 1959 was dissatisfied.†

Democracy in Malaya faces several obstacles, the most im-

* National elections to the House of Representatives must be held at least every five years, but can be held sooner. Some senators are elected by the state legislatures, and others are appointed by the paramount ruler; all hold office for six years, half of them assuming office every third year.

† Malaya's Chinese community is divided in many ways, including politically. The exclusively English-speaking Chinese (of the "older families"), the wealthy businessmen, the pro-Peking and pro-Formosa elements, and the Chinese who speak various different dialects are among the more conspicuously identifiable groups.

BERNALD LIBRARY
COLBY JUNIOR COLLEGE
NEW LONDON, NEW HAMPSHIRE

portant being the existence of exclusive racial communities. A related question concerns the favored constitutional position of the Malays (for government posts and other benefits) and the pro-Malay policies of the ruling Alliance Party.

However, Malaya, like the Philippines, seems to have established democratic institutions that work. Both nations face essentially the same problem: the utilization of these institutions for the benefit of the whole population.

### Indonesia

Indonesia, which—like its ethnically related neighbors, Malaya and the Philippines—started out with democratic political intentions, presents a sharp contrast to these two countries in terms of the establishment of viable representative institutions.

Indonesia became independent in circumstances completely different from those surrounding the peaceful births of free Burma, Malaya, and the Philippines. The Indonesians had to fight their Dutch colonial rulers for independence for four bitter years. During these years, the would-be independent republican government, proclaimed on August 17, 1945, in the wake of Japan's surrender, functioned under a hurriedly prepared constitution that was never intended to be anything more than provisional. This constitution gave the republic's President, the nationalist patriot Sukarno (his only name, although some writers have added an incorrect first name of Achmad), greater power than he was to possess legally under subsequent charters.

A second temporary constitution was adopted following the Hague Conference in late 1949 that resulted in Dutch recognition of Indonesian independence. This charter made Indonesia a federal state and provided for a national government of democratic form. Less than eight months after its adoption, the federal charter was replaced by another constitution which, although otherwise similar, made Indonesia a unitary government. Indonesia probably should have had a federal structure, in view of the extensive geographical dimensions of the island nation and the ethnic and linguistic differences among its people. But federalism was a Dutch idea, and the Indonesians were suspicious of it.* Even so, the unitary government was supposed to be provisional; early elections were anticipated for a constituent assembly to draw up a new permanent constitution. However, these elections were not held until December, 1955.

The lack of cabinet leadership, the multiplicity of parties and the differences within them, the emergence of extraparty (and extralegal) political institutions, the dimensions of the problems to be solved, and general inexperience in self-government are the principle reasons for Indonesia's failure to make democratic institutions work. Also, Indonesia provided for a dual executive, and this has probably been the main structural source of its governmental difficulties. Dual executives have not posed a major problem in the other lands of South and Southeast Asia (except Pakistan), probably because the chiefs of state in these countries have not been their nations' most important political figures. India's president, for example, enjoys nothing resembling the prestige of Prime Minister Nehru—and Burma's president is not as powerful as Prime Minister Nu. The difficulty in Indonesia can be traced primarily to Sukarno. The 1950 constitution made the president something of a figurehead, and this is a role Sukarno is temperamentally unsuited to fill.

At the beginning of its independence in 1950, in fact, Indonesia had both a European-style parliamentary government and a powerful president. The legislature was the single-chamber House of Representatives, from which the prime minister and cabinet were ordinarily selected and to which they were responsible. Up until 1955, however, the House was democratic only in the sense that Indonesia's national leaders, in allocating to themselves seats in the parliament, probably reflected the popular feelings of the country as accurately as they could without holding elections. Although there is no doubt that Sukarno was, and

* This is not to say that the federal approach would have prevailed except for the fact of Dutch endorsement. Various Indonesians have criticized federalism as both economically unworkable and politically disastrous for their country because Indonesia as an integral whole can only develop "when plus and minus areas help each other," as First Minister Djuanda has put it. The issue is no longer a current one in Indonesia, but is of contemporary significance in such African countries as Nigeria and the Congo.

is, the most popular political personality in the country, and that he could probably be elected president now if an election were held, the fact remains that he was never voted into office. The other revolutionary leaders simply chose him as president when offices were allocated in 1945.

For the first ten years of its proclaimed freedom, Indonesia's national government lacked popular endorsement through anything like an election. Sukarno's behavior during these years was frequently arbitrary and beyond the scope set for the president by the 1950 constitution, but he was not then generally recognized as an insurmountable barrier to the establishment of democratic government in his country. Indeed, it was widely felt both inside and outside Indonesia that the country's political instability could be largely corrected by national elections. The people would choose their rulers, and with such a mandate, the prime minister and cabinet of the majority party, or of a coalition majority, could get down to the task of solving Indonesia's mounting problems.

The elections, though they were free and drew heavy participation, failed to work a miracle. Four parties—the ultrasensitive Nationalists, the moderate and somewhat pro-West Masjumi (modernist Islamic), the conservative Moslem Scholars, and the Communists—obtained 198 seats (57, 57, 45, and 39, respectively) in the 260-member House of Representatives. This lack of consensus in support of any single party or program did nothing to alter the existing Indonesian pattern of weak coalition governments. The president, according to the 1950 constitution, was supposed to act only on the cabinet's advice, but Sukarno was even less disposed to do this after the 1955 elections than before.

So alarmed did some anti-Sukarno elements subsequently become at the President's behavior, including his apparent pro-Communist drift and his economic policies toward the outer islands (particularly Sumatra), that they rose in revolt against the central government. A "Revolutionary Government of the Republic of Indonesia," with a leading Masjumi politician as prime minister, was proclaimed in central Sumatra on February 15, 1958. The revolt still smolders, but it is not a threat to the survival of the state, since it was quickly contained by the army.

However, regional grievances had preceded the 1958 revolutionary effort—and they have continued in its wake.

The evolution of Indonesian political institutions following the Sumatran revolt veered even more sharply from the democratic path. However, the direction in which the country was moving was no clearer than the interrelationship of the many governmental institutions that were established in these years. So jumbled organizationally was Indonesia's government in the late 1950's and early 1960's that President Sukarno's speeches gave the impression that even he did not know exactly how many major governmental organs there were or what they were all doing.

In 1960, after discarding the Constituent Assembly and unilaterally (and illegally) proclaiming a return to the "strong president" 1945 constitution, Sukarno also dismissed the elected House of Representatives. He replaced it with an appointed body of quite limited authority, which was supposed to be subordinate to a 609-member Provisional People's Congress. Only two powers existed above himself, Sukarno declared in June, 1960: the Congress and Allah; but the membership of the Congress, described by the President as the nation's highest governmental authority, was appointed by him. In addition to the Congress and the House, Indonesia also has a Cabinet, an Inner Cabinet, a Supreme War Council, a Supreme Advisory Council, a National Planning Council, and a National Front. The pyramidal Front, extending down to the village level, gives every appearance of being an official national party.

Despite this array of institutions (appointive, rather than popularly chosen), Sukarno unquestionably runs the country today. He does not, of course, blame himself for Indonesia's political difficulties—the short life of the cabinets, the unsolved problems, and the frequent resort to violence. Nor does he attribute the shortcomings during the 1950's to Indonesian unreadiness for democracy or his own tendency to advocate ad hoc decision-making, thus bypassing the legislature. The fault, Sukarno says, is in democracy itself, which cannot cope with the problems of resurgent Indonesia. Political parties have been the main source of Indonesian disunity, Sukarno has stated, but he does not mention that he has deliberately played off party against party or that Indonesia's problems seem to have become worse with the decline of its parties in recent years.

Of the four Southeast Asian countries that have tried to establish democratic governments in the postwar period, Indonesia is the only obvious failure. The blame cannot be placed on representative government. The Indonesians tried, though not very hard—and President Sukarno hardly tried at all. The democratic institutions of the Philippines and Malaya may not have produced the most satisfactory policies, but they work; those of Burma have been through very trying times, but they survive. In Indonesia, however, democratic institutions have passed from the scene.

### Thailand

Change in the institutions of government is also taking place in Thailand, which flirted a bit with democracy in the early postwar period, but never progressed to the point of a serious love affair.

Thailand was never ruled by a colonial power. The object of the revolution in 1932 was to displace an oligarchy—that is, the royal family—with a group of civilians, mainly professional persons and civil servants, and soldiers, who wanted to participate in running the country. It was a revolt to reduce the power of the ruling class, but it was not a democratic revolt. It did, however, establish a quasi-parliamentary constitutional monarchy, with the king as head of state.

The 1930's, far from being democratic years, ended on an authoritarian note—in imitation, however imperfect, of the Japanese, Germans, and Italians. The wily Field Marshal Phibun Songkhram came to power as Premier in 1938, but, because he cooperated with Japan, he had to leave office when the fortunes of war changed. He was succeeded (in fact, if not at first in form) by his long-time chief civilian rival, Pridi Phanomyong, and a period of instability followed, with nine governments in three years.

Pridi had stronger democratic inclinations than Phibun, and

parliamentary elections were held in 1946, but the population, unaccustomed to being consulted by its leaders, did not turn out in large numbers. Democracy's prospects in Thailand, if it really had any, were eclipsed the next year, when Phibun and the army staged a comeback coup.

The coup of 1947 inaugurated a new era of military dictatorship, although Phibun was now less dominant a figure. The crafty soldier-politician held office during the first seven years of the 1950's largely because he was able to maintain a delicate balance between the army and the army-like national police. Phibun, as Prime Minister, together with his Cabinet, was constitutionally responsible to the single-chamber House of the People's Representatives, but since he had appointed half its membership, the responsibility was clearly limited. In a transparent bid for the political support of liberal sentiment against his main adversaries, he did introduce a couple of pseudodemocratic institutions during his second period in office—an American-style press conference and a Thai version of London's famed Hyde Park—but these got out of hand and were dropped. Phibun was unseated in September, 1957, in another coup, led this time by his army chief, Sarit Thanarat.

Sarit, already the actual political boss for more than a year, became Prime Minister in October, 1958. He had gone abroad for medical treatment, but then flew home suddenly to execute what amounted (figuratively) to a coup against himself. His immediate and loyal army deputy, General Thanom Kittikachon, the Prime Minister since Phibun's ouster, had not been able to maintain effective political control of the country. So Sarit staged his "revolution," as he called it, and subsequently handpicked a Constituent Assembly to draw up a new constitution and establish a De Gaulle-style presidency, with severely limited responsibility to the legislative body.

### The Indochinese States

Like Thailand, the Republic of Vietnam (South Vietnam) cannot honestly be considered a country that has tried to establish democratic government. A unitary state with a democratically oriented constitution and a national government theoretically separated into executive, legislative, and judicial branches, it has a strong presidential system, or rather a dictatorial version of one. The president possesses such power and has used it in such a way that South Vietnam's government is not very different from that for which Thailand seems to be aiming.

The South Vietnamese president is directly elected by universal suffrage and secret ballot. He holds office for five years and can be re-elected for two additional terms. On paper, as well as in practice, he dwarfs the single-house National Assembly, which, although elected directly by the people by secret ballot for a three-year term, is, nevertheless, composed exclusively of supporters of President Ngo Dinh Diem because the candidacies are controlled. To date, the Assembly has been nothing more than a rubber stamp for President Diem's policies. The third division of the government, the judiciary, has not been any more independent, despite its description in the constitution as a separate branch of the state structure.

President Ngo Dinh Diem has ruled the country autocratically ever since he came to power, after the 1954 Geneva partition. As Premier in 1955, Diem held a referendum and replaced Head of State Bao Dai as President. In the August, 1959, elections he evicted the only opposition member elected to the 123-man Assembly. The action was not untypical and illustrates the controlled environment of Vietnamese government and politics. Diem was re-elected over only token opposition in April, 1961.

The governments of Cambodia* and Laos—two other states formed out of what was once French Indochina—have structural

---

* It can be argued that Cambodia should be included with the group of four states that originally experimented with democratic government. Cambodia's was, in fact, a multiparty system until 1955, and its governmental institutions are still nominally democratic in form. However, in view of the brevity of the experiment (independence having been finalized only in 1954) and the lack of real opposition to its early abandonment, it is felt that Cambodia should not really be included in the four-nation group. There has never been the degree of support for democracy in Cambodia—let alone an understanding of it—that has characterized the Philippines, Malaya, Burma, or even Indonesia.

similarities, but operated in markedly different ways in the years 1954-60. The Lao were ruled by a premier-cabinet type of government that functioned inadequately when it functioned at all.

Laos' king is its nominal chief executive. Of the two-house national legislature, only the fifty-nine–member lower house, the National Assembly, is important; the upper chamber, the non-elective King's Council, has only nominal authority. The prime minister is technically responsible to the National Assembly, but this relationship was practically meaningless in the late 1950's and early 1960's.

"Democracy," Laotian-style, has been characterized mainly by *coups d'état*, rigged voting, and civil war of the sort that flared so sharply in 1960-61. There has been an unmistakable resemblance between government in Laos and the old parlor game of musical chairs.

Governments have changed frequently in Cambodia, too, but for quite different reasons. Prince Norodom Sihanouk, political stalwart of the country, has popped in and out of the premiership in the past like a jack-in-the-box, but his political importance in the country has not fluctuated correspondingly. Prince Sihanouk stepped down as King in 1955 in favor of his father, partly to demonstrate his belief that premiers were more important than monarchs.

Cambodia's premier and cabinet, though technically responsible to the legislature, are actually handpicked by the Prince and accountable to him, no matter what office he holds. The parliament, like that of Laos, is bicameral: The sixty-one–member lower house, the National Assembly, is the more important chamber, but generally does not initiate policy, while the upper house, the Council of the Kingdom, is a royal advisory body. The Assembly cannot be regarded as an institution where policy alternatives are really debated because all its seats are held by the Prince's People's Social Community Party. The legislature is clearly subordinate to the executive, who in turn is subordinate to Sihanouk, who does not always occupy a formal position in the government. This, however, has not prevented votes against the government of the day in the National Assembly—even to the point of precipitating cabinet crises. But the crises are always resolved in concert with the views of the dominant Prince Sihanouk.

In terms of personalized rule, the government of North Vietnam (also formerly part of French Indochina) is the very opposite of Cambodia's, despite the prestige of the venerable Ho Chi-minh. North Vietnam is a Communist state, and it is the Party that rules. The governmental structure, like that of China, includes a dual executive: President Ho Chi-minh and Premier (and Foreign Minister) Pham Van Dong. President Ho, the chief of state, was long the driving force behind the Vietminh revolutionaries who defeated the French in a bloody civil war. Ho and Pham can be compared to Mao Tse-tung and Chou En-lai of China in the period before Mao resigned as chairman of the Party in favor of Liu Shao-chi: Ho is the aging and near-legendary national leader, while Pham is the government's managing director.

Like other Communist lands (and some non-Communist, as we have seen), North Vietnam also has a facsimile legislature, a single-chamber National Assembly, for which elections were first held in January, 1946, prior to the start of the eight-year war between France and the Vietminh. Many of the deputies died or left the Assembly before the next elections were held in May, 1960, and North Vietnam's legislature during most of the period since partition has been a kind of rump parliament, if it has been a parliament at all. The Assembly, which the constitution calls the highest organ of state authority, met only eleven times during the decade and a half between elections.

The 1960 voting, like the balloting in any Communist country, was a mockery of the principle of the popular selection of governments; there was no doubt that the Communist Lao Dong (or Workers) Party would continue to control the state. Balloting was not secret, and there were contests for only one-third of the seats. Four minor parties participated in the elections, but theirs was only a propaganda role, as part of the government's effort to convince doubters inside and outside North Vietnam that free political association is allowed.

**Singapore**

Singapore—unlike North or South Vietnam, Thailand, Cambodia, or Laos—has attempted democratic government and has done a creditable job of making representative institutions work, even though the state is not yet fully independent. Singapore began internal self-government in 1959, while Britain retained responsibility for foreign and defense affairs. The constitution inaugurating the new governmental arrangements is scheduled to be reviewed by the two countries before 1963. Like Malaya and Burma, the two Southeast Asian nations to which the United Kingdom has already given independence, Singapore is ruled today by a parliamentary-style government, with a prime minister and cabinet collectively responsible to an elected fifty-one–member Legislative Assembly. A head of state and representative of the British Crown called the *Yang di-Pertuan Negara*, an independent judiciary, and a seven-member Internal Security Committee are the other main organs of government. Three Singapore, three British, and one Malayan representative sit on the Committee; their duty is to deal with matters of internal security that have both internal and external implications. The ruling People's Action Party, which won forty-three of the fifty-one seats in the 1959 Legislative Assembly elections, with 54 per cent of the popular vote, is a party of the left; its present leadership is democratically oriented and has made representative government in Singapore successful to date.

✿    ✿    ✿

Communist North Vietnam stands at one extreme as the least democratically oriented of the contemporary governments in Southeast Asia. The Philippines, Malaya, Burma, and the not-yet-independent Singapore, on the other hand, have governments that are democratic in form and, to varying degrees, in fact. Indonesia, Thailand, and South Vietnam cannot be regarded as democracies by any criteria. Cambodia claims to be a democracy, but like its even more underdeveloped neighbor Laos, it has been governed since independence by a veritable handful of men.

The fact that the Philippines and Malaya are two of the most stable and prosperous countries in the region today, with bright prospects for the future, seems to support Burmese Premier U Nu's view that democracy has a relevancy for contemporary Southeast Asia. But the obstacles to democratic government in Southeast Asia remain many—among them, political inexperience, the lack of democratically oriented leadership, high illiteracy rates, the Communist challenge, and low living standards. Despite such obstacles, however, democracy has started to work in two of the countries, the Philippines and Malaya, and possibly in Burma.

# Three

# THE SEARCH FOR THE
# APPROPRIATE POLITICAL SYSTEM

PRESIDENT SUKARNO has termed democracy "inappropriate" for Indonesia. Many Southeast Asians do not share his outlook, but there is a widespread feeling that independence has not been all it should have been, partly because of existing political systems. This is why there has been so much talk of modifying these systems, why alterations in present institutions have been proposed, and why some changes have already taken place. A search for what Sukarno has called "the appropriate" in political institutions is in progress. It is a search that developed in the second half of the 1950's and gained momentum in the early 1960's.

### Indonesia

Sukarno, who represents an anti-Western and antidemocratic outlook, has turned his back on Europe and the United States as sources of institutional inspiration for government in Indonesia. He has stated that he is seeking a system "in harmony with the Indonesian soul," one in which "there will be no debating and examining points against one another that can result in the dissolution of the House of Representatives or the return of the mandate of the cabinet." What Sukarno wants instead is a government based on the traditional Indonesian ideas of *musjawarah* and *mufakat:* all interested parties discuss a problem until they are in agreement; no vote is ever taken.

But what if the participants cannot agree? In such an eventuality, Sukarno told his hand-picked legislature in June, 1960, the matter should be referred to him.

Sukarno calls his "concept" (as he terms it) "guided democracy," or "democracy with leadership," which seems like an almost grudging recognition on his part of the continuing popular appeal of the idea of democracy in his country. "The heart of the guiding in a guided democracy," he has said, "is deliberation, but a deliberation that is guided by the inner wisdom of perception." Although there is no question about his recent consistent opposition to political parties and majority rule, Sukarno appears to lack a clear idea of what form guided democracy should assume—except that he should do the guiding.

In 1957, when Sukarno first revealed his concept, guided democracy was to include a new high advisory "national council," headed by himself, and an all-party cabinet, including the Communists. This consultative council was both to supplement and partly to supplant the elected House of Representatives as a major policy-making organ of government; it was to function according to Sukarno's nonvoting formula. The all-party cabinet, for its part, was to be a body that was not dependent on parliamentary support, one in which party interest and advantage were forgotten, and one that would, in effect, be led by Sukarno himself. There was considerable opposition to Sukarno's concept, which he claims came to him in a dream; those who were most critical were the anti-Communists, particularly the Masjumi and Socialist parties.

Finding himself opposed, Sukarno demanded a return to the short and flexible 1945 constitution, which gave more power to the president. The Constituent Assembly would not meet this demand, so he dismissed the Assembly; when the legislature proved unwilling to function within the unilaterally restored 1945 basic law, he "deactivated" the legislature. This wholesale housecleaning of legitimate government was preceded, accompanied, and followed by the introduction of the new institutions previously described (in Chapter 2), including what seems to be shaping up as an omnibus official party, the National Front.

The Front's potential role in Indonesian political life has been likened by some of Sukarno's critics to that of the Communist Party in a Marxist state. Other parallels also have been drawn between Sukarno-style guided democracy and government in Communist lands. The fact that Sukarno proclaimed, "I have seen the answer," after he returned from Communist China in 1957, and simultaneously began his efforts to establish guided democracy in Indonesia is not without significance.

This is not to suggest that Sukarno is a Communist working for the establishment of a Chinese- or Soviet-style state in Indonesia. However, he may be borrowing institutions from the Communists—a single national party (the National Front) and the Inner Cabinet (a small decision-making body similar to the Central Committee)—in an effort to "retool," as he puts it, the Indonesian national revolution. His short-term objectives certainly seem clear enough; he himself said, in 1959, that he wanted to rule for five years "without interference of the opposition." That is why, besides being President, he is also Prime Minister, commander of the armed forces, and "control authority of the state of danger."

Sukarno has his critics, although some of them are no clearer than he about the kind of government they want. Several of the groups opposed to the President have joined together in the Democratic League, which is not really a party. Politicians associated with the conservative Moslem Scholars, the Catholic and Protestant parties, and the banned Masjumi and Socialist parties may be found in the League, which has so far been very cautious, for Sukarno today wields extraordinary powers over all political activity. Another group supporting the League is a body called the Independence Upholders, in which there is strong army representation.

Three aims characterize the Democratic League: a return to an elected parliament, a limitation of the executive powers possessed by the president, and a reduction of the strength of Communism in the country and Communist influence in the government. Sukarno's willingness to accept Communist support, his continuing unconstitutional enlargement of his own powers, and his dismissal of the Constituent Assembly (in 1959) and the

House of Representatives (in 1960)—both elected bodies—place him squarely in opposition to the objectives of the League.

The Democratic League, as its name implies, would like another and more determined try at democracy in Indonesia. Besides its political and military supporters, the League is also backed by a sector of the bureaucracy, certain educational and intellectual circles, and some members of the increasingly harassed press. It appears to regard itself—and probably rightly so—as representing the rational and the modern in a struggle against Sukarno's highly personalized and traditionalist-oriented leadership. The only major parties not in any way associated with the League are the Nationalists and the Communists—the former closely allied with Sukarno, and the latter possessing distinct objectives of their own, although supporting Sukarno in the short run for tactical reasons.

The Communists were at first enthusiastic about guided democracy, presumably because they saw in it an opportunity to increase their own influence over the government. As a result of army pressures, however, guided democracy became markedly less advantageous to the Communists between its 1957 unveiling and Sukarno's efforts in 1959 and afterward to implement it. The Communist leadership today is not sure how much it can trust President Sukarno, who seems to incline alternately toward the Communists and toward the army. But the Communists are sure about one thing: their own ultimate goal. They have a quite specific answer to the search for the appropriate.

The most important obstacle facing the Communists is probably not Sukarno, despite his continuing prestige, but the 200,000-man army, led by the able but not always decisive General Abdul Haris Nasution. Nasution, frequently mentioned as a possible replacement for Sukarno, publicly stated his approval of his chief's new powers and the multiplicity of new organs as being "in agreement with history and the Indonesian personality." "The democratic concept we practiced in the past," he said, "was not consistent with the personality of the Indonesian people's heritage since ancient times."

The army is the largest of Indonesia's three services. Basically anti-Communist, it is keenly aware of its political importance.

Some of its leadership, associated with the Independence Up-holders and the Democratic League, clearly supports the West-ernized democrats. General Nasution does not, but he is something of a political enigma. He has alternately revealed himself as a kind of rival to Sukarno and as one of the main props of his regime.

Regardless of Nasution's role, there is no doubt that the army as an institution will be an important factor in the governing of Indonesia for a long time to come. It could, indeed, come up with its own answer in the search for the appropriate: military rule, à la Thailand.

### Burma

If democracy has a chance in Burma, it is because U Nu believes it appropriate for his country. Nu held out as Premier in the worst days of the multifactional insurrection in 1949, although some well-known figures left his government. He re-signed his office in 1957 to purge his political party of corrupt and antidemocratic elements, a task that proved too big in the face of resistance from other leading members of the party. His courageous opposition to the army during the eighteen months of military rule and his spirited speeches in support of democracy during this period contributed in a major way to the return of civilian government and a second try at democracy.

Yet, Nu has been critical of the functioning of the would-be democrats, including himself. After he returned to office in April, 1960, he established a five-man senior advisory committee, headed by former President Dr. Ba U, to help the government avoid the kind of mistakes that characterized the old freewheel-ing days before the AFPFL split. Power had gone to the heads of the politicians, who were inexperienced in democratic proce-dures, Nu stated during the 1960 campaign—and this had been true of himself as well. In his speeches of recent years, Nu has also recognized the impossibility of truly democratic government without an effective parliamentary opposition, but his own Union Party (the "clean" faction of the AFPFL) scored such an overwhelming victory in the 1960 elections that its majority, which includes its allies among the representatives of the indigenous minorities, is today greater than that of the old united AFPFL. Nu admitted, moreover, that in the first decade of independence the politicians had acted too frequently without consulting the main interested groups in Burmese society. He promised in the 1960 campaign to hold a series of conferences for politicians, government officials, and other Burmese concerned with various areas of government activity. Burma's government after British withdrawal, Nu and others recognized, had bit off more than it could chew. The goals of industrial-development and social-welfare projects were too ambitious to be fulfilled. Perhaps, if its objectives in its second attempt at democracy are more modest, it will succeed or come closer to succeeding than in the past.

Although it may be too early to judge the leadership of the new Nu government, first signs are not encouraging. Student pressures in 1960, following the return of Nu to the premiership, forced him to undo, for all practical purposes, the efforts of the intervening military regime to raise academic standards at the University of Rangoon. It is this same lack of effective leadership that characterized government in Burma in the first decade of independence. Under that leadership, all students taking the high-school matriculation examinations were passed after a student was killed in a demonstration protesting an alleged leak of examination questions through a Rangoon newspaper; illegal squatter huts were built indiscriminately on the outskirts and in various parts of the capital city, without government interference; prices and the flow of goods to the market could not be controlled. Democracy in an underdeveloped country of limited personal and mass discipline (as Burma is) seems to require a particularly skilled kind of leadership, and some say that Nu cannot supply it.

U Nu is not only Burma's leading democrat, but also its foremost traditionalist: He publicly propitiates the *nats* (the spirits of Burmese animism) and consults regularly with astrologers. It was Nu who promised in the 1960 election campaign to make Buddhism the state religion; he has also proposed time off for civil servants to retire to the pagoda for Buddhist meditation.

Part of the explanation of Nu's great public appeal is that he is a religious hero to the people—some say, a Buddha in the process of becoming. In his dual role as traditionalist and democrat, Nu may bridge the gap between the old and new in ways that Indonesia's antidemocratic Sukarno cannot. However, he may be trapped by the less compromising traditionalism of some of his followers, thus jeopardizing democracy's future chances in Burma.

Besides the democrats and the traditionalists, the two other groups who could significantly influence the future government of Burma are the Communists and the army. The Communists (and other insurrectionists) seriously threatened the survival of the government in 1949-50, but since then the Communist rebels have been forcibly relegated to a nuisance status. Despite the fact that the legal Communist party, the National Unity Front, was almost obliterated in the 1960 elections, Communism as an ideology continues to be a major challenge to the country. It has a hold on many of the politically alert students at the University of Rangoon, which is the prime breeding ground of the nation's intellectual elite.

Although the Burmese military toppled the civilians from power in 1958, the present army leadership is probably more democratically oriented than General Nasution and some of his associates in Indonesia. The 1958 coup resulted from the deterioration of security conditions in the country; the army felt that the situation posed a major threat to its own and the nation's survival, but after removing this threat, it restored the civilians to office in April, 1960.

The commander-in-chief, General Ne Win, more than any other single person, was responsible for the army's exemplary conduct in relinquishing power after fulfilling its caretaker responsibilities. There is little doubt that it took Ne Win's immense prestige to carry some of the other officers with him. Like Indonesia's democrats, Burma's army leadership is anti-Communist, antitraditionalist, and strongly attached to Western administrative practices; but its democratic orientation has limits. If the army ever returned to control of the governmental machinery again, it would undoubtedly set up a military dictatorship, however enlightened, that would last longer than eighteen months.

The search for the appropriate in government is a vital pursuit in Burma, although it has not been accompanied by the mass of institutional innovations that have characterized Sukarno's quest in Indonesia. The numerically small but important Rangoon professional class, unimpressed with the performance of U Nu and the other civilian politicians in the old AFPFL days, clearly found the military rule of General Ne Win the most palatable kind of government it has known since independence. So did many intellectuals, and more civil servants than would care to admit it now that U Nu has returned to power. Nor is the army itself convinced that the present political arrangements ought to be perpetuated. Premier Nu is, in a very real sense, on trial with the military.

### Thailand

The institutions of pseudodemocratic complexion that have been established and re-established in Thailand since the revolution of 1932 have been virtually meaningless. There has been a parliament—and a prime minister and cabinet, too—but no really democratic government. If the intentions of ruling strongman Field Marshal Sarit Thanarat are correctly understood, the Thai constitution now in the process of formation will be even less democratic (but perhaps more realistic) than the half-dozen other charters the country has had during the last quarter-century.

Field Marshal Sarit is impressed with the kind of strong presidency established by France's General Charles de Gaulle. He allegedly wired the Thai Embassy in Paris for a copy of the De Gaulle constitution as soon as it was available, then instructed his hand-picked Constituent Assembly to produce a basic law characterized by at least as vigorous and independent an executive. The Constituent Assembly is expected to bring forth a constitution with a president independent of the legislature and also a parliament with power to delay but not initiate legislation.

It is unlikely, however, that even such strong executive government could cope adequately with all, or even most, of the serious problems of Thai political procedure. The president under the new constitution will be selected by some formally defined process, but such constitutional provisions for designation of the prime minister existed in the past. The Thai method of filling the country's top political post, however, has been the *coup d'état*, and it is difficult to see how this device can be institutionalized—or eliminated—given the political ambitions of the Thai military (Sarit Thanarat and Phibun Songkhram are good examples).

If free elections are to be part of the new Thai system, it is difficult to see how political leadership by the military can be assured—or how civilian control of the military can be developed, if the latter exert their influence mainly by indirect means. Thailand is not oversupplied with democrats or able civilian politicians, but it has some, such as former Premier Khuang Aphaiwong. Uncontrolled elections probably would return Marshal Sarit as the first president under the new constitution, but this cannot be assured—nor can it be assured that the outcome of future balloting would be accepted by the losing faction.

Most observers feel that Sarit is sincere in his intention to avoid the corruption of past Thai governments, but it is doubtful how much genuine support for these aims he enjoys among his own military supporters, particularly among the ranks of the comparatively young and ambitious. For example, will soldiers stand for election to the legislature or, for that matter, to the presidency? If a civilian were elected president, would he be free to nominate nonmilitary figures to the top posts in his administration?

These questions are especially important in a country like Thailand, where many young men have entered upon military careers not because they wanted to be soldiers, but because it is necessary to rise through the military hierarchy to achieve power and position. It is difficult to imagine a peripheral role for so many men of ability and ambition.

With the exception of the premiership and a few cabinet portfolios, the leading Thai military personalities do not themselves hold the top policy-making and administrative posts in the government today. But they are in a position to influence the official decision-makers, and they are rewarded in a variety of ways. Traditionally, the Thai military has preferred to rule through civilian positions, particularly in the civil service. Senior officers are found in abundance on the boards of directors of governmental and quasi-governmental economic enterprises, receiving high salaries and sometimes shares of stock and having use of company automobiles, secretarial help, and the like. They also are frequently asked by private businesses to accept appointments to their boards of directors or to serve as nominal executives—thus ensuring for the enterprise friendly treatment by the government.

The long-range future of Thailand poses a real question. Marshal Sarit's constitution-makers will be doing their nation a major service if they can produce a basic law that provides for orderly succession and for a government corresponding to the political realities of the country. Then the way will be cleared for possible future development of more popular, as well as more stable, rule.

"We cannot copy wholesale the Western ideas of constitutions or the Anglo-Saxon forms of democracy," Deputy Speaker Sanya Thammasak of the Constituent Assembly has said. "We have to find the kind of democracy that will be right for Thailand. This is the same problem facing all Far Eastern nations—which type of democracy will work in our countries? We accept that democracy is the best form of government, the best way of life. But how can we approach it best with respect to our traditional way of life and our concepts?"[*]

Thailand's apparent answer is offered with an eye more toward tomorrow than today.

## South Vietnam

Governmental and political change can really occur only by forcible means in South Vietnam, where the legislature is controlled, the press muzzled, and free political parties nonexistent.

[*] Quoted in *The New York Times*, July 24, 1960. The Deputy Speaker said essentially the same thing to the author, when he visited in Thailand.

Opposition to President Ngo Dinh Diem's regime can be expressed only by violence, and this is what happened in November, 1960, when 3,000 paratroopers, led by Colonel Nguyen Chanh Thi, rose in armed revolt against Diem. For nearly twenty-four hours, the rebels controlled the capital city of Saigon and held Diem a virtual prisoner while they negotiated with him. Diem's courage never failed, however, and arrival of loyal troops turned the tide of victory in his favor.

It is not clear whether Diem's survival was a setback or a victory for democracy's prospects in Vietnam. Some of the supporters of the rebels were associates of Bao Dai, at one time the puppet emperor backed by the French and hardly a democrat. President Diem, on the other hand, despite the character of his rule, has given several indications that he intends to democratize the government. He is said to have modeled his Vietnamese regime structurally on the American national government for two main reasons: a desire for strong executive leadership more likely to come from a presidential than from a parliamentary system and the hope that such a structure could some day be transformed into a genuinely democratic government.

The abortive 1960 revolt was not the first serious sign of dissatisfaction in South Vietnam. A manifesto, drawn up by several anti-Communist leaders (including ten former cabinet ministers), had been issued six months earlier, charging that Diem's policies had "only oppressed the people, not protected them from Communists." This was the same charge made by the rebel military committee, which stated in a broadcast: "Ngo Dinh Diem adopted a family dictatorship and was unable to face the situation, which was deteriorating because of mounting Communist danger. The army has been divided, and the population is without any freedom."

The Communist threat was real enough, as evidenced by the stepped-up activity by agents of Ho Chi-minh's North Vietnam regime in the preceding months, but the motivation for the attempted coup seems to lie elsewhere. Anti-regime (but anti-Communist) politicians Dr. Phan Quang Dan and Tran Van Van and certain soldiers, including Colonel Nguyen Chanh Thi and Lieutenant Colonel Vuong Van Dong, apparently acted to displace the existing ruling group, to participate in the governing of the country themselves, and to liberalize the regime. Their attempt may be regarded as part of the same post-independence search for the appropriate in political arrangements that is taking place elsewhere in Southeast Asia. The rebellion failed, but the search continues.

It is not the structure of government that is under attack in South Vietnam, but rather its utilization. So personalized is Diem's administration, however, that the government and the man (and his relatives) seem inseparable. Moreover, President Diem is a firm man—rigid, some say. There is serious doubt that he will bend before he is broken. But if he is broken, government in South Vietnam could be quite different. Whether it would be different in structure is not certain. Nor is it certain that the government would be less authoritarian; revolutionaries frequently assume the shortcomings of those they have supplanted. One thing is certain, however—President Ngo Dinh Diem and family are sitting on a powder keg. There will be another explosion; it is simply a question of when.

More serious than the likelihood of Diem's ouster—and, given his vigorous anti-Communism, this would be a serious matter for the rest of Southeast Asia—is the possibility of internal strife in South Vietnam. Much, but not all, of the army is loyal to Ngo Dinh Diem personally, as the abortive coup showed, so fighting within the army is a distinct possibility. And from such a split, only the Communists would benefit.

The possibilities facing South Vietnam, in the order of their probability, are: first, military rule on the order of Thailand; second, Ngo Dinh Diem's continuation in power; third, a more liberal parliamentary regime, which might be short-lived; and finally, a Communist takeover, instigated by North Vietnam, whose agents continue their efforts to weaken and supplant the government of the southern portion of divided Vietnam.

## Laos and Cambodia

Communism, which seriously threatened South Vietnam at the start of the 1960's, could become a greater menace to that state in the near future as a result of the gains it has registered in neighboring Laos during late 1960 and early 1961. Lacking a democratic tradition (like both South Vietnam and Thailand), backward and divided Laos has also lacked determined leadership of the sort Ngo Dinh Diem has given his country, the kind of crude stability that characterizes Thai politics (despite frequent recourse to the device of the *coup d'état*), or even the most rudimentary technical and administrative skills. There was nothing in the record of Laos between 1954 and 1960 to suggest the feasibility of democratic political institutions for the once French-ruled kingdom.

The military successes of the Communist Pathet Lao rebels and their neutralist allies in 1961—which effectively divided the country—provided only the most recent evidence that parliamentary institutions are unlikely to have an opportunity to develop in Laos in the foreseeable future. The civil war of 1954-57, the army coup of January, 1960, the rigged elections in April of the same year, and the subsequent seizure of power by paratrooper Kong Le in August had already cast ominous shadows across the Laotian political horizon. Moreover, the split within the army between the anti-Communists and the neutralists had eliminated the military in mid-1960 as a force for stability in the country.

Parliamentary institutions were adopted in Laos primarily because the country had to have some kind of government and this was the system existing in France, the retreating colonial master. The size of the National Assembly, the lower and more important chamber, was enlarged in 1958, but this was the closest the country's non-Communist political leaders came to re-examining the constitution prior to the outbreak of civil war in 1960. There is really no quest for the appropriate in governmental arrangements in Laos—only a rough-and-tumble struggle for power.

The possibility of the ultimate establishment of a Communist government over all of Laos is a very real one. In December, 1960, the right-wing military forces of General Phoumi Nosavan regained the capital of Vientiane from the Communist Pathet Lao and army elements supporting Captain Kong Le, but a dramatic reversal in the fortunes of the anti-Communists followed in the first months of 1961 as the Soviet-supplied Pathet Lao insurrectionists gained control of half the country. These light-ning-like shifts of fortune of the various contestants for power—the high drama of coup and countercoup—revealed the instability of Laotian politics at their most dangerous. The stakes in Laos are considered high by both the United States and the Sino-Soviet bloc (including North Vietnam). It is possible that Laos' future governmental arrangements will be decided essentially by forces beyond its borders.

In many ways, Cambodia could not be more different from Laos. The future form of its government has been the subject of frequent consideration—but largely by one man and his advisers, including court astrologers.

Prince Norodom Sihanouk made a major impact on the consti-tutional evolution of Cambodian government in 1955 when he resigned as King. His occupancy of the premiership might have stimulated the development of parliamentary rule if it had been continuous and had given to the office (as contrasted to the man) the position of leadership in Cambodian politics. The strength of Sihanouk's party, the People's Social Community, in the parliament also gave him the means to set a precedent for effective govern-ment of the premier-cabinet type. The fact that Cambodia's premiers have been, in effect, the political servants of Sihanouk has downgraded the office. However, the Prince "agreed" in June, 1960, to assume the position of Chief of State. This gives him a second opportunity to influence favorably the shape of Cambodian government.

For all his jumping in and out of office, Prince Sihanouk has shown considerable interest in the democratization of Cambodia. He has traveled widely in the country to meet the people and explain government policies—although his junketing seems much like a Renaissance court on tour. "You must remember that the people will eventually decide the fate of the underdeveloped countries," he says,* and there is no question that he believes it, despite his personalized rule. Sihanouk has sought to prevent the development of a conservative government clique, like the one that controlled Laos during 1954-60, which would be totally out

* Quoted by Denis Warner, "The Prince on the Tightrope," *The Reporter*, XXII (February 18, 1960), pp. 32-34.

of contact with the masses. He has even decreed periods of manual labor for government officials, in imitation of Communist China.

At the moment, young Sihanouk (thirty-nine) can hold practically any office he wants and pursue almost any policy imaginable; he is that popular and that powerful. Nor does he face an immediate Communist problem comparable to that of Laos or Vietnam. But a major burden rests on his shoulders. He can significantly influence his country toward democracy or encourage a cult of personality that will leave his people unprepared for the day when he is no longer their ruler.

### Lands Less Likely to Change

The Philippines, Malaya, Singapore, and North Vietnam are less concerned with the search for new institutions of government. But the Filipino nation does face the major problem of making its democratically oriented institutions more democratic, while Malaya and Singapore—formerly ruled as a single unit, for all practical purposes, by the British—are confronted with the problem of their future relationship.

The Philippines has American-style democratic institutions, but these do not work in the American manner (not that they should entirely). The basic problem seems to be that the aspirations of the common man, particularly the rural masses, are not reflected in government policies. The Philippines is probably most accurately described as a democracy in the process of becoming, with the advantage of representative institutions already in existence. There is no question of the adequacy of these institutions, except among the small minority of Communist sympathizers. The problem is essentially the one confronting all young democracies: the enlargement of participation of the governed in the governmental process.

Both Malaya and Singapore, like the Philippines, incline strongly toward democratic government. Constitutionally, the major problem of the future for these two lands—independent Malaya and internally self-governing Singapore—is the nature of their relationship. Although Singapore has never been part of Malaya, it was linked with that land in all but formal constitutional ties. This *de facto* association of the colonial period became a casualty of Malayan independence, although the two territories still maintain various ties.

Singapore, which has a population of 1.5 million, wants to become part of Malaya, which has about 6.8 million inhabitants, but the Malays of Malaya strongly oppose such a move. Their reason is obvious enough: Malaya's Chinese minority is a large one as it is, but with the addition of predominantly Chinese Singapore, there would be more Chinese than Malays. Today, half of Malaya's population is Malaysian (including Indonesians as well as Malays); with Singapore's Chinese, Malaysians would constitute only 41 per cent of the inhabitants, while 44 per cent of the country's residents would be Chinese (the remaining 15 per cent would comprise other Asians and Europeans).

Malaya's Prime Minister, Tengku Abdul Rahman, has repeatedly ruled out the possibility of any merger. Malaya's efforts to establish a rubber market in its capital city of Kuala Lumpur to supplant Singapore's, its policy of developing industries to reduce its dependence on Singapore, and its expansion of Port Swettenham as an alternate port leave little doubt as to the Alliance government's intentions. But Singapore's government continues to seek some kind of association.

Besides the question of its future relationship with Malaya, Singapore is also faced with the problem of leftist extremism. The ruling leftist People's Action Party, led by Prime Minister Lee Kuan Yew, on the whole a responsible organization, has its extremist elements. The future role of the radicals (such as fiery labor leader Lim Chin Seong) is tied up with the problem of relations with Malaya. The establishment of some kind of link with the Malayan Government would be a positive accomplishment for the present PAP leadership and would help to undercut the extremists' position.

North Vietnam, like most of the other lands of the area, will probably undergo change of some sort in the future, but major governmental alterations are not likely immediately. Moreover, such change as the future brings will probably move the North Vietnamese further along the road to becoming a fully Communist state.

The new 1960 North Vietnamese constitution gives the president more power than most Communist charters do, with the prime minister serving, in effect, somewhat like the premier in De Gaulle's Fifth French Republic. There is a parallel here with the trend toward a stronger executive in some of the other nations of Southeast Asia, although it is possible to exaggerate the significance of this likeness in view of the Communist character of North Vietnam.

*    *    *

In Southeast Asia, the 1960's started out as a decade of political change. Indonesia experienced a wholesale institutional reshuffling as President Sukarno sought to establish his "guided democracy"; Thailand drew up a new basic law; and Malaya and Singapore struggled with the problem of their future constitutional relationship. The initial years of the 1960's were also years of political violence, as evidenced by the rapidly shifting developments in Laos and the accelerated Communist guerrilla activity and the attempt to oust President Diem in South Vietnam.

The dominant characteristic was the apparent drift toward strong executive government. This was what President Sukarno sought in Indonesia, and Field Marshal Sarit in Thailand. Burma, too—in fact, if not by constitutional change—had a stronger executive under General Ne Win during 1958-60 than previously, under Premier U Nu.

The *coup d'état*, long a mainstay of Thai politics, became the means of succession elsewhere in Southeast Asia. Since 1957, five countries—Burma, Thailand, Laos, South Vietnam, and Indonesia—have experienced rebellions, successful or otherwise. In each of these rebellions, all or some of the leaders were military men, an indication of the increasing involvement of military personnel in the nonmilitary aspects of government.

The trend in both the forms and practices of government in the early 1960's appeared to be away from democracy. How long and to what extent this trend will persist is, of course, unknown. However, there is a strong belief in some quarters that democracy and its related paraphernalia, such as elections and political parties, have had their day and been found wanting. This is not always overtly stated, as it was by President Sukarno in Indonesia, but the feeling is there.

Four

# THE POLITICAL PROCESS

POLITICS in Southeast Asia today utilizes only a very limited percentage of the potentially available resources at the national political level. The character and manner of operation of political institutions, governmental and otherwise, differ considerably from those of the West—as, indeed, do many of the purposes of contemporary political activity. The various arenas of politics in these lands are only loosely integrated, if at all, while the governments that are at the core of the various political systems are unstable in most cases.

## Political Parties

There are political parties in all the countries of Southeast Asia (except Thailand, where they have been banned). However, only the parties in the Philippines, Malaya, Burma, and Singapore are free. In North Vietnam, there is only one party, the Communist Lao Dong (Workers) Party, although nominally there are two other "parties," the Socialists and the Democrats. (Two additional organizations participated in North Vietnam's May, 1960, elections: the "Patriotic Buddhist" and the "Resistant and Peace-Loving Catholics" associations.) In South Vietnam, political parties as such are not forbidden, but they are carefully controlled.

In Indonesia, where no fewer than twenty-eight parties won seats in the 1955 elections (twelve capturing only one seat each), there are still eight officially allowed parties, but these do not include the two most important ones opposed to President Sukarno in the past—which he has now banned. Cambodian Prince Norodom Sihanouk has also restricted those parties that he considered likely to end or alter his rule. Elsewhere, only the Communist parties have been outlawed—as in Malaya, Burma, and the Philippines. The Burmese, however, have permitted the continued existence of a pseudo-Communist party calling itself the National Unity Front. The Laotian Patriotic Front was similar to Burma's NUF, but the former conservative government of Laos chose to terminate its political freedom—a contributing factor in the recurrent crises in Laos in the early 1960's.

The explanations of the present limited importance of political parties are varied. In all the countries of Southeast Asia, there are strong antidemocratic forces: Indonesian President Sukarno is opposed to Western-style liberal democracy, as is the army in Thailand (of which Sarit Thanarat and Phibun Songkhram are the most illustrious products); and in South Vietnam, a continuing Communist threat against a government presided over by a dedicated but autocratic ruler has discouraged the development of free parties. In short, the cards have been stacked against political parties (as they are understood in the West).

On the other hand, some of the parties and their leaders have been extremely provocative—even threatening state security. The Philippine Government outlawed the Communist Party, but only after the Hukbalahaps had resorted to violence. At least some members of Indonesia's banned Masjumi and Socialist parties also were associated with a revolt against the state.

A major problem in several of the countries is the diverse character of such parties as do exist. The most conspicuous example of an excessively multifaction party was the Anti-Fascist People's Freedom League of Burma. The AFPFL was created in 1944 as an omnibus nationalist coalition to drive out the Japanese and win independence from the returning British. It included nationalists, Communists, socialists, opportunists, and any other group or person willing to join the anticolonial struggle under its banner. After World War II, it split—not once or twice, but several times. Thakin Soe's Trotskyite Communists broke away; subsequently so did the Than Tun–led Stalinists, some of the resistance fighters associated with the Peoples Volunteer Organization, and the "Red Socialists" (the pseudo-Communists who had stayed behind when Than Tun's group rose in armed revolt). Then, in April, 1958, the main body of what was left of the party split into factions led by Prime Minister U Nu on the one hand and Deputy Premiers U Kyaw Nyein and U Ba Swe on the other.

The AFPFL, formed to obtain liberation from colonial rule and later transformed into a government party to socialize the country, foundered because it did not reflect genuine unity, nor could it compromise the differences among the leaders of its several factions. Much the same thing has happened to some of Indonesia's parties, though on a lesser scale, and this explains why Indonesian parties have also been unable to cooperate across party lines in pursuit of larger common goals, as they did in the struggle against Dutch domination. The same fate may await Malaya's ethnically fragile Alliance or Singapore's People's Action Party (in which a wide variety of leftists are active).

Other parties in Southeast Asia, such as the People's Social Community Party of Prince Norodom Sihanouk in Cambodia, represent only the personal followers of particular individuals. Some, like the now-defunct National Socialists of Thailand's Marshal Sarit Thanarat, have been no more than devices for absorption of potential opposition. Burma's Communist-oriented National Unity Front has been only a loose electoral alliance. Indonesia's National Front is regarded by its critics as an official arm of the regime that will increasingly dominate the political life of the country as a control device. Only the free parties of the Philippines, Malaya, and Singapore are stronger than the men who currently control them—though of course some of the Communist parties do loom larger than their leaders.

The roles played by parties vary from country to country. Some of the parties remaining in Indonesia are more political nuisances than anything else, while others serve only as feeble reminders of alternatives to Sukarno-style government. But even the boot-licking Nationalist Party has virtually no influence in the making of governmental decisions in Indonesia today. In Burma, on the other hand, parties were at least useful as devices for organizing the followers of the competing leaders and conducting the campaigns for the February, 1960, elections. President Ngo Dinh Diem in South Vietnam utilizes parties—if the National Revolutionary Movement or the Revolutionary Party may be considered parties—as devices of control and the means of giving the appearance of popular support to his authoritarian regime. A major function of Malaya's Alliance to date has been to keep the country's diverse races from fighting one another, politically or otherwise. Only in Malaya, Burma, the Philippines, and Singapore have parties formed governments and assumed responsibility for policy formation and execution.

Parties have failed, for the most part, in at least five ways to make democratic government possible and effective in Southeast Asia: They have not provided leadership; they have not been able to hold together in the face of the demands placed on them by independence; there have been too many of them; they have lacked real roots among the people; and they have been motivated more by the desire for survival of particular inner party groups or individuals than by the urge to solve the pressing problems of the day.

The Philippines is the only country in which a two-party system has developed since independence. In most of the other countries, there has been no room for responsible Western-style opposition; and the opposition that has existed has been expressed in such extralegal actions as the 1958 Sumatran revolt in Indonesia or the civil war in Laos.

The fact is that political parties, as known in the West, developed in particular environments in Europe, and in those countries settled by Europeans, that have not been duplicated in Southeast Asia. Parties in several of the Southeast Asian countries seem to be artificial devices grafted over an alien political culture. They undoubtedly serve important political purposes, though these not only vary from country to country, but the functions of parties also are different from those usually associated with the Western organizations of the same label.

**Interest Groups**

The activities of the interest groups in Southeast Asia reflect the character and structure of the diverse national societies— the differences in value systems, salary levels and cost of living, recent history, literacy, development of communications, etc. In some of the countries, they are likely to resort fairly quickly to violence, partly because of the more limited means of expression available in lands with low literacy rates, limited newspaper audiences, and comparatively few radios.

Those interests seeking to influence policy are not all formally organized, and even where they are, they may not be primarily organized for political purposes—and further, those organized for political purposes are not always organized for the same kinds of immediate purposes or in the same structural fashion as such interests are in the West. On the whole, such groups are not as autonomous as they are in the United States. For instance, there are labor organizations in Burma, but they are primarily adjuncts of the political parties, such as U Nu's Union Party, the anti-Nu "stable" faction of the once-united AFPFL, or the pro-Communist National Unity Front, each of which has its own "union."

These unions exist not to seek economic and political goals desired by their membership, but as a means of maximum partisan direction of the political activity of labor.

Much of the activity aimed at influencing public policy involves government groups—civil servants and soldiers. This sector of the population is much more important in Southeast Asia than in the United States—a reflection, in part, of the socialist policies of several of the national governments, policies that have made civil servants of persons who would be privately employed in other countries. Governmental or semigovernmental interest groups seem least important in the Philippines and Malaya, the two countries with strong traditions of nonpartisan civil servants and soldiers, with more developed national economies, and with comparatively stable party structures as well as democratic governments.

Interest groups in Southeast Asia also differ from those of the

West in terms of the way they act (and are used) in the political processes of their lands. Not only are groups used by the parties, but they are also much more frequently exploited by the governments as instruments of national policy than in the United States. A number of them, for example, have been stimulated to action by Indonesian President Sukarno as a method of fulfilling some of his anti-Dutch objectives.

Because many potentially politically important groups are not yet aware of the ways in which they can actively influence policy, they play no conscious role in the political process—or, at best, only a very limited one. Frequently, the goals sought by some groups, particularly those new to politics, are surprisingly noneconomic in nature. Indeed, some of the activity is not directed toward the pursuit of any defined objective, but merely represents a sector of society expressing its frustrations just for the sake of doing so. Many of the interests that do play a part in the political process, moreover, are very general, such as those reflecting the widespread but ill-defined yearning for economic development.

The activity of interest groups, like that of political parties, is probably more important in the Philippines than in any other country in the area. This stems from the more developed political consciousness of the Philippines, as well as its greater economic diversity—which, of course, brings with it conflicts of economic interests. The Philippines is primarily an agricultural nation; it grows, among other products, coconuts, sugar cane, abaca, tobacco, and rice. There is considerable competition among the different agricultural interests that also takes the form of intraregional rivalry as a result of area specialization in certain crops. Moreover, the Philippines is sufficiently developed so that these interests have acquired organizations for political action, such as the National Federation of Sugar-Cane Planters.

Indonesia also is conspicuous for the variety of its competing interest groups—although not all of them are effective in getting what they want from government. The explanation for the limited significance of parties and the much greater importance of interest groups in Indonesia would seem to lie in the fact that parties are less functionally appropriate to the political environment of the country—which never actually resembled Western lands as much as its formal governmental institutions seemed to suggest. Moreover, Indonesia's economy is variegated and is characterized by area specialization that is exaggerated by the insular geographical character of the country, with resulting quite defined regional economic interests.

There is a significant amount of organized group activity in Malaya and Singapore. Malaya has its important rubber and tin interests, an increasingly organized labor force, and (probably the most important of its competing groups) its Malay, Chinese, and Indian ethnic communities. Thailand, Burma, South Vietnam, Cambodia, and Laos (more or less in the order listed) have much less organized economic group activity than the other countries of the region.

There are politically active groups, of course, other than those with economic interests and goals. The Peoples Volunteer Organization, the military force formed by Burmese nationalist Aung San to aid in gaining his country's independence from the British, became a veterans' group afterwards. Almost everywhere in Southeast Asia, the army is extremely interested in public-policy formulation and execution, and it is the single most important organized group in Thailand, Burma, Indonesia, and South Vietnam. The other armed services are also important as political interest groups in some of the countries. Thailand's navy made a major effort to seize control of the government from the army at the start of the 1950's, and the air force and navy are both forces in the multicornered Indonesian political struggle. Ethnic minorities (including aliens and Eurasians), royalists (in Thailand, Cambodia, and Laos), and religious groups (Moslem, Buddhist, and Christian) comprise other groups interested in influencing public policy in Southeast Asia today.

An increase in efforts by various interests to participate in the political process may be expected in all the Southeast Asian countries as such interests grow and become more organized and politically oriented. Meanwhile, some of the governments give less than adequate expression to even some of the more important interests in their countries. The underdeveloped role of economic and other interests in Southeast Asian politics today can be considered a major cause of the shakiness of the various national regimes.

## Public Opinion

Public opinion is expressed quite differently in Southeast Asia than in the West. Both the symbols employed to influence public opinion and the institutional means available for the expression of the views of various sectors of society are affected by the belief structure and the technology of the countries in question. Informal communications processes, such as those involving Buddhist monks and laity in Burma, are probably more important than the Western-style media, but their workings are little known in the West.

Systematic surveying of mass opinion is virtually nonexistent as a factor of political importance. Polls have been conducted by a few newspapers, but these apparently have not particularly influenced either the readers or the politicians. There is no question, on the other hand, that astute politicians like Burma's U Nu or Malaya's Tengku Abdul Rahman try to keep their finger on the pulse of the people by whatever means are available to them. Indeed, it has often been said that U Nu is too much a creature of public opinion as he understands it: In the summer of 1958— before the army takeover of September-October—Nu even organized a series of national seminars to tap the opinion of major sectors of the population. Cambodian Prince Norodom Sihanouk has sought in his own way to find out what the people think by making periodic tours of the countryside, taking a large part of his court (and the diplomatic community) with him.

Elections have been an important barometer of public opinion in the Philippines, Burma, Malaya, and Singapore, although elsewhere they have not usually been free enough to serve this purpose. The smashing presidential victory of Ramón Magsaysay in the Philippines in 1953, besides being an endorsement of Magsaysay the man, provided vigorous proof that the Philippine people wanted a government with which they could indentify themselves and their interests. Similarly, the overwhelming election of U Nu in Burma's February, 1960, voting was as much a protest against the rigorous reformism of General Ne Win's army caretaker government as it was a show of confidence in the widely revered Nu. Even in Thailand, where elections have been such a mockery, the voting of March, 1957—whose first undoctored returns revealed the unpopularity of the Phibun regime—gave army chief Marshal Sarit assurance that he would not meet with public opposition if he moved to topple the government.

The press is not of major importance as an indicator of public opinion in Southeast Asia, except in the Philippines, where the newspapers do reflect the views of the numerically limited but politically important upper middle class. This limited role of the press is hardly surprising in countries with such high rates of illiteracy and where the overwhelming majority of the population lives in inaccessible rural areas. In any case, the press in most of these countries is not free and thus cannot even accurately mirror the views of an informed minority. Indonesia and Cambodia have several times closed down newspapers for the expression of unpopular opinions, while South Vietnamese editors are told daily which news is fit to print. Self-censorship of the press exists in Thailand and is no less restrictive because of its "voluntary" character. Although the press has sometimes shown itself to be courageous in Burma, it displayed real timidity under the government of General Ne Win. Only in the Philippines, Malaya, and Singapore can the press be considered free, and even in the latter two lands there are indirect controls.

One of the most effective expressions of public opinion in Southeast Asia, as in many other underdeveloped areas, is through demonstrations, violent or otherwise. Burma has had its share of demonstrations by monks, students, and refugee squatters for a variety of reasons, one of which has been U Nu's tolerance of such activities. Not so very long ago, the People's Action Party, which today governs Singapore, was deeply involved in strikes, riots, and even murders. Presumably, such methods of expressing public opinion and seeking to influence government policy will become less important as institutions are developed through which aroused sectors of society can more peacefully express their views.

**Ideology**

Unquestionably, the most important ideological force in Southeast Asia today is nationalism. Its theme is essentially the same everywhere: the transcendent importance of a particular people and their national political unit. Burma's Thakins, youthful nationalist agitators of the 1930's (among whom were U Nu, Aung San, and the Communist Than Tun), loudly proclaimed their theme of one nation and one race. Indonesia's *Pantja Sila* (five principles), first formulated by Sukarno in 1945, include nationalism as one of the five pillars of the state, and it has become increasingly clear that this is the most important principle in Sukarno's thinking.

Another principle of the *Pantja Sila* is social justice (or socialism, as it may be ideologically translated for many Southeast Asians), a major political influence in Burma and Singapore, too, as well as almost everywhere in the region. Communism, which is not unattractive to many Southeast Asians, provides the theoretical foundation, or (perhaps more accurately) rationale, of the North Vietnamese political system and is an ideological force in all the other countries.

Democracy was an integral element in the pre-independence nationalist revolt against colonialism, but as an ideology is probably less significant in Southeast Asia now than at any time in the last quarter-century. It is an important force today only in the Philippines, Burma, Malaya, and Singapore. Belief in the equality of all men, which means Asians and Europeans more than it means Burmans and Karens or Malays and Chinese, and the belief that economic modernization is the answer to the desire for a better life are other important ideas that help to shape the substance of politics in Southeast Asia. These ideas, however, are largely the contribution of the former ruling Western powers.

There are several indigenous political concepts, too. Two of these are *musjawarah* and *mufakat,* part of President Sukarno's guided democracy. *Musjawarah* means "consultation" and *mufakat* "decision" in the sense of "communion" (like the Quaker approach). Both *musjawarah* and *mufakat* are probably more important as part of the intellectual framework of contemporary

Indonesian politics than is the Western concept of representative government.

Islam, as the traditional religion of the country (for longer than the period of Dutch dominance, anyway), is also an integral part of Indonesian politics. Sukarno, a Moslem, is a secularist in terms of his ideas about church and state, even though he listed faith in God as one of the *Pantja Sila*. But the leaders of the banned Masjumi Party have sought a socialist state that would at the same time embody the ideas of Islam. The Moslem Scholars, another major party, holds even stronger views on the contemporary political relevance of Islam. And the Dar-ul Islam insurrectionists waged a civil war against the government as part of an effort to establish a Moslem theocracy in the country.

Buddhism in Burma, Thailand, Cambodia, and Laos is even more politically potent than Islam in Indonesia or Malaya. Burma's U Nu, as the Buddhist leader in politics, seeks to fulfill various tenets of his faith through his official position. The government's sponsorship of the Sixth Great Synod of Theravada Buddhists during 1954-56 was largely Nu's doing. Some of Nu's economic and social-welfare ideas also have at least some of their roots in his Buddhist thinking. The economic well-being of the people, for example, would give them more time for religious meditation and good deeds. Already the state religion in Thailand, Cambodia, and Laos, Buddhism is in the process of becoming that in Burma. In Thailand, Buddhism is virtually synonymous with nationality in the sense that many Thai find it difficult to think of a person as being Thai if he is not Buddhist.

The ideas of particular men also play significant roles in Southeast Asian politics. Sukarno's guided democracy is the most conspicuous example. The philosophic "personalism" of President Ngo Dinh Diem, in which the free personality achieves maximum development as an active and helpful member of the national community, is an important factor in South Vietnam. Field Marshal Sarit was able to persuade many people in Thailand that his second coup of 1958, displacing a hand-picked premier, was a "revolution," a move for major change, and not just the latest version of the Thai habit of changing governments.

**Rule by the Individual**

Probably the single most important factor in the political processes of Southeast Asian countries today is rule by the individual. This is obvious in such cases as the dictatorships presided over by Indonesia's Sukarno and Thailand's Field Marshal Sarit. But it extends further—to leaders like Burma's U Nu and Cambodia's Prince Norodom Sihanouk, who play extremely important roles in their countries without being dictators or petty tyrants. In short, government by the individual (if it may be called that) is far too complex a phenomenon to be explained wholly in terms of dictatorial or semidictatorial political institutions or of personal ambitions.

It clearly has its roots in ancient times, as well as in the period of European colonialism. Before the West began to dominate the region, government was largely personal, as is revealed in the history and mythology of the various Southeast Asian lands, in the accounts of such heroic but domineering figures as Bayinnaung and Alaungpaya of Burma, Indonesia's Gaja Mada, Vietnam's Gia Long, the Jayavarmans of Cambodia, and Thai monarchs Mongkut and Chulalongkorn. During the colonial era, the government *was* the governor or governor-general. It is therefore not at all surprising that the experience of a strong personal leadership for so many years should have had at least as great an impact upon the present political orientation as the limited example of parliamentary rule supplied by the restricted colonial legislatures and the alien notion of democracy gained chiefly from books.

The three lands where personal rule is least important today, interestingly enough, are those countries that lack a history as a single unit and where colonial rule was as impersonal as anywhere in Southeast Asia—the Philippines, Malaya, and Singapore. The Philippines was not a unified country before the coming of the Spaniards in the sixteenth century. And Western rule, Spanish and then American, lasted for several centuries, as contrasted with the less than sixty-five years of British rule over Burma. The American governor in the Philippines never had the power of his British counterpart in Burma, nor did he use what power he did have as vigorously. Indeed, during the tutelary Commonwealth period, which began in 1934, the effective head of the Philippine Government was the elected Filipino President, Manuel Quezon.

Malaya was not a united political entity at any time in the pre-Western past either. It did not really become a single unit until the establishment in 1948 of the Federation of Malaya Government, although its separate parts did function somewhat as a whole under the prewar arrangements of the Federated Malay States, Unfederated Malay States, and Straits Settlements. British policy toward Malaya was designed to continue traditional Malay institutions, which meant a less important overt role for the Crown's representatives. Equally important, Malaya had no tradition of a strong common ruler like Alaungpaya in Burma or Gaja Mada in Indonesia.

Singapore, also a British creation, was ruled as part of the Straits Settlements, together with Penang and Malacca. It was subject to the same general influences as Malaya.

The historical experiences of these three countries contrast sharply with those of the other nations of Southeast Asia, which had a tradition of strong individual leadership and were subjected to a more heavy-handed brand of colonialism. The Dutch in Indonesia and the French in Indochina were represented by much more forceful governors than the Philippines or Malaya ever knew under the Americans or the English. There was even a great difference between British Burma and British Malaya.

Other factors help explain why government by the individual characterizes Southeast Asia today. Burma's U Nu, for example, dominates Burmese government not only in the pattern of past strong indigenous leaders, but also in harmony with the Burmese concept of the moral or religious leader. Nu's hold on the Burmese people—and on Burmese government—is not maintained by force, nor is it wholly the result of political skill, which he possesses in abundance. It is partly a matter of moral leadership, with the Burmese giving deference to and bestowing power upon a man who fits their idea of the truly good Buddhist. On the other hand, the position of Marshal Sarit Thanarat in Thailand, although consistent with the tradition of domineering leadership in his country, can be largely explained in terms of his control of the army, a condition that has elevated individuals to positions of political control in most countries of the world at one time or another.

A final consideration stems from the unsettled character of the political process. When political parties or the legislative institutions of governments are not by themselves strong enough to carry the burden of the first independent years, the Sukarnos, Nus, Sarits, Sihanouks, and Diems fill the leadership vacuums. They or someone else are likely to continue to do so for some time to come—until less personalized methods of government develop.

### Decision-Making

In the days before the split in Burma's AFPFL, the important political decisions were made by the party's executive committee. The party leaders who comprised the fifteen-man committee were a kind of oligarchy in the sense that they were responsible to only a handful of professional politicians. Premier U Nu was unquestionably the most important single person in the group, which he tended to dominate by the force of his prestige and personality rather than through sanctions. Sometimes, he made decisions on his own—and though they may have been discussed and even attacked at the committee meetings, they were never reversed.

There is no question as to who is responsible for the important decisions in Thailand today: Marshal Sarit makes the largest share of them himself, and he probably dominates the political process as much as any single individual in Southeast Asia today. He holds power as a result of his leadership of the army, over which he has been able to maintain control so far, apparently without being appreciably influenced by it. There are no parties in Thailand, and no other interest groups have a major impact on Thai policy. Before Sarit took over from Phibun in 1957, the country was governed, for all practical purposes, by a group analagous in function to Burma's AFPFL executive committee;

it was called the Coup Group and was composed of the participants in the major coup of 1947.

President Ngo Dinh Diem makes the decisions in South Vietnam. Diem delegates somewhat more authority to others than does Sarit, but these others are usually either relatives (particularly brothers Ngo Dinh Nhu and Ngo Dinh Can) or close friends. Because he sees himself as the man who can save his people from the tyranny of Communist slavery, Diem's leadership is understandable only within the framework of this dedication and self-image. There are groups whose interests he must keep in mind, but they do not influence the shape of his goals. The army, for example, is both the main instrument employed by Diem to rule the country and an organization whose interests must be at least partly satisfied. He keeps the army subordinated by his direct contact with the field commanders and by rotation of personnel to prevent the development of cliques within the military.

Prince Norodom Sihanouk must also be regarded as the most important single policy-maker in his country. Indeed, in some ways he is an even more dominant figure than Sarit or Diem, because Cambodia is more underdeveloped and there are fewer interests seeking to influence the decision-making process. There is, for example, no group in Cambodia to compare in significance with the Thai military or the South Vietnamese Army.

President Sukarno, of course, is the single most important decision-maker in Indonesia, but he is not as much in control of the situation in his country as are Prince Sihanouk, Marshal Sarit, and President Diem in their lands. Sukarno is boss, but he is boss partly because of his adroitness in maintaining an effective balance among competing factions. Probably the single most important group influencing Sukarno today—and one that he has cleverly kept at arm's length—is the army, which is basically anti-Communist and therefore sets a definite limit to the freedom Sukarno can permit the Communists. The army probably has not moved against him because Sukarno has given it just enough of what it wants; moreover, there is sufficient rivalry within the army itself so that Sukarno can manipulate the various military factions, playing them off one against the other.

The Communists have clearly influenced Sukarno to the extent that he has failed to take action against them, thus giving them what they want in the short run—the opportunity to keep boring away at the solidarity of the state.

The army has been successfully held in check in Indonesia, but not in Laos. Since the 1954 Geneva settlement, the army's influence over ever-larger areas of public policy has increased. In the first years after Geneva, the army was a major prop of the anti-Communist regime and the main instrument of the government in fighting the Communist Pathet Lao rebels. The strong showing of the pro-Communist candidates at the polls in May, 1958, frightened the Laotian conservatives, however, including some of the army leadership. The right-wing Nationalist and Independent parties coalesced to form the Rally of Lao People, and younger and conservative government officials, including some army officers, established the anti-Communist Committee for Defense of the National Interest and the allied Paxasangkhom Party. The CDNI was a strong influence on the 1959 conservative government of Prime Minister Phoui Sananikone and became even more powerful after the death of the able Deputy Premier, Katay Sasorith, in late 1959.

The army coup of January 1, 1960, set up a caretaker regime that rigged the subsequent April elections, permitting pro-CDNI candidates to win throughout the country. The army itself was split, however, as illustrated by the August, 1960, coup led by neutralist Captain Kong Le, and the subsequent civil war that made Laos a major concern of the great powers in late 1960 and 1961. The division in the army's ranks, indeed, was probably the decisive internal factor tipping the balance in favor of the Communists. The fact that Communists, neutralists, and conservatives found themselves seeking to advance their respective causes by military means in 1960-61 is testimony itself to the importance of soldiers in the Laotian political process.

The political processes in the Philippines, Malaya, and Singapore, although each is different from the other, are even more different from the politics of the rest of the region. The Filipino political leadership is basically democratic in its orientation and follows parliamentary procedures. Interest groups exist in abundance and include all the major commodity producers as well as organized labor, schoolteachers, and the Catholic Church. The Filipino press probably is more influential in helping to shape public policy than any other in Southeast Asia. In short, although the Philippines is unquestionably an underdeveloped country, it is closer to the more advanced nations elsewhere in the world than most of the Southeast Asian lands.

To a certain extent, this is also true of Malaya, where the Alliance Party affords the main means for resolving differences among the various ethnic groups. Singapore is, in effect, a one-party state because of the overwhelming preference of the electorate for the ruling party. It is the party leadership that makes the important decisions, with Prime Minister Lee Kuan Yew the most important decision-maker (though by no means on the scale of Burma's Nu). Organized interests, such as government workers and unions, influence policy in Singapore, but the People's Action Party has run directly counter to their wishes when necessary.

We do not really know how decisions are reached in Communist North Vietnam, but the political process there seems similar to other Communist satellite countries. The Lao Dong Party is the main internal decision-making instrument, but it is clearly subordinate to both international Communism and North Vietnam's neighbor Communist China.

❈    ❈    ❈

In general, the political process in the Southeast Asian nations may be divided into three major categories. North Vietnam is in a category by itself as the only Communist country in the region, although it could be joined by Laos in the near future. Thailand, South Vietnam, and Cambodia are nations with, for all practical purposes, one-man rule. Indonesia falls more into this category than any other, but President Sukarno is more restricted by interests than is Marshal Sarit, Prince Sihanouk, or President Diem. In the Philippines, Malaya, and Singapore, the major interests and the parties largely direct the political process. Burma under U Nu (though he is democratically oriented) is closer to the second category than the third in the sense that major interests really do not determine public policy; instead, Nu himself makes most policy, but not as a Sukarno- or Sarit-type dictator.

As has already happened in the Philippines, Malaya, and Singapore, the political process will undoubtedly become more formalized and increasingly complex in future years; at the same time, it is likely that interest groups (military, economic, or ethnic) will assume more importance than a single leader. But this does not necessarily mean that the formal structures of government will be liberalized overnight. That is a goal for the long-term future.

FIVE

# THE USES OF GOVERNMENT

THE COUNTRIES of Southeast Asia, like most of the lands that have recently gained independence from colonial rule, are "have-not" nations in comparison with the economically developed West. The United States accounts for about 40 per cent of the world's income with only 6 per cent of its population. Southeast Asia, the home of 7 per cent of the world's inhabitants, accounts for less than 1.5 per cent of total world income (and only one-thirtieth the annual American income). The contrast is more significant in view of Southeast Asia's abundance of mineral resources and fertile soil.

No country in Southeast Asia is yet industrialized, although most of these nations are trying to become so. There is practically no heavy industry in the area, and light industry is nowhere sufficiently developed to meet ordinary consumer needs. The percentage of the working population engaged in manufacturing pursuits or related activity is highest in the Philippines, but even there it is less than 12 per cent; in Malaya it is under 8 per cent, and in Burma less than 2 per cent. The trading patterns of these countries also indicate how economically underdeveloped they are. Everywhere, food and mineral products are exchanged for manufactured items ranging from heavy equipment to a wide variety of consumer goods. For example, petroleum, rubber, and tin are Indonesia's leading exports, with textiles, machinery, and transport equipment among its main imports.

Although Southeast Asia is not faced with region-wide population pressures nearly as staggering as those of neighboring India and China, some of the countries have definite population problems, while parts of others are overpopulated. For instance, the population of Indonesia has increased by almost 50 per cent since 1930, and the number of inhabitants in the Philippines grew by about 25 per cent during the first decade of independence. The annual rates of population increase for Malaya, 2.7 per cent, and the Philippines, 2.5 per cent, compare with 1.7 per cent for the United States and 1.1 per cent for Japan.

The Red River delta region of Communist North Vietnam has one of the highest population densities in the world: about 1,500 persons per square mile. Java, Indonesia's most populated island (with two-thirds of the country's inhabitants in an area of 51,000 square miles) has a population density of 314.5. Singapore, the Philippines, and Malaya also face rapidly rising population densities.

This expansion of populations means that more food must be produced or imported—or less eaten. The major component of the Southeast Asian's diet is rice; protein foods are more or less a luxury. Burma's production of rice had reached prewar levels by the late 1950's, but exports were off by one-half because of increased consumption within the country. Neither the Philippines nor Indonesia, both predominantly agrarian countries, has yet to achieve self-sufficiency in food production, despite years of effort, while Malaya is the Southeast Asian land most dependent on external food sources. The average daily per capita caloric intake in the United States is 3,244 units; for Burma, it is 1,986, for the Philippines 1,980, and for Indonesia 2,045. (The minimum requirement for existence is generally regarded as about 2,000 units.)

Inadequate food represents only one of the many health problems facing the new Southeast Asian nations. Dysentery, tuberculosis, malaria, and other diseases have afflicted large segments of the populations, and there is an acute shortage of doctors, nurses, hospitals, and medical supplies; for example, Indonesia has one doctor for every 60,000 persons, as contrasted with one for every 710 Americans.

These are only a few of the pressing difficulties that face the newly independent Southeast Asian nations. There are problems of land ownership in some countries (in the Philippines, for example, where only half of the farmers own all the land they work) and of the size of land holdings (as in Indonesia, where the average farm holding on Java dropped from 2.45 acres in 1930 to 2.2 acres in 1955). Illiteracy is a common problem throughout the area; the adult illiteracy rates are 35, 45, and 62 per cent, respectively, for the Philippines, Indonesia, and Malaya —and more than 90 per cent for Laos. Moreover, in some countries, sizable segments of the population do not speak the national language: Malaya, for example, has a large Chinese minority that has shown only limited interest in learning Malay; in the Philippines, Tagalog (the main Filipino dialect) is understood by only 35 per cent of the people, and English by about 30 per cent. Equally important political, social, and economic problems also exist in connection with unassimilated minorities, internal security, transportation and communications, electric power, animal breeding, and capital formation.

Some of these problems, like those dealing with health, are age-old ones for the peoples of Southeast Asia; others, such as population growth and the need for corresponding or greater increases in food production, are in part the result of recent European colonial rule. There is increasing awareness in practically all these countries that not all people in the world are as badly off as themselves, and this poses serious problems of a political character. The nationalist leaders in the struggle against their imperial rulers capitalized on the desire for improvement, and the hour of independence brought with it the need to translate promises into accomplishments—which they have not done.

## Economic Policies

The differences that exist in the uses of government are most evident in the varying approaches toward the question of economic organization—i.e., public or private ownership of the main institutions of the economy and the role of the state in the distributive process. The avowed objective of the political leadership of some of these countries is the establishment of a socialist state. This is easy enough to understand. The former metropolitan powers were capitalist countries, and during the era of imperialism the men who are today's leaders were exposed to the Marxist explanation of colonialism in terms of the inevitable shortcomings of capitalism. Capitalism is an anachronism, they read (or were told), and socialism is a higher type of economic organization, more humane and egalitarian (characteristics that particularly endeared it to young men smarting under the inequalities, real and imagined, of colonialism). More important, socialism seemed to them a better means for the task ahead. The economies of the Southeast Asian lands were underdeveloped; there was so much to be done that progress was possible only with governmental ownership of the main economic institutions. The job of industrialization, diversification, and modernization was so big that only government could be big enough to take it on. Only government could mobilize the limited resources, financial and human, of these lands. Socialism would also help to diminish foreign control of the economy and give the nation economic independence to match its political freedom.

This was the way Burma's young leaders thought in the first years of independence. Premier U Nu and his associates in the ruling Anti-Fascist People's Freedom League had long dreamed of the day when they could nationalize the big British enterprises and reduce the hold of the iniquitous Indian moneylender and landowner over the Burmese peasantry. Independence gave them their chance. They quickly took over the British-owned Irrawaddy Flotilla Company, which controlled almost all the inland water transport in prewar Burma. One-third of the country's timber concessions were immediately nationalized, and state monopolies were created for such purposes as the export of rice, the country's main product. The government also moved to redistribute the land to the cultivators, although it was handicapped in this by its limited physical control of most of the country as a result of the several-sided insurgency in progress. Elaborate currency controls were instituted, and the government assumed direction of exports and imports through its allocation of licenses. The AFPFL leadership also sought to modernize the economy by establishing new industrial and manufacturing enterprises. Rice revenues were to be used to industrialize the nation, and, with the help of foreign aid, it would be no time, Premier U Nu and others said repeatedly, before Burma was a modern and self-sufficient industrial state.

The role of government in the economy, as viewed by Nu and his associates, was not that of mere regulator or controller. The government was to operate the main economic institutions itself. The establishment of a socialist state as a means of economic development and as an instrument of social benefits and equality was an avowed Burmese aim. A number of British firms were allowed to remain, under varying restrictions, and the Indian and Chinese minorities continued to dominate large sectors of the commercial life of the country, but they were supposedly living on borrowed time.

More than a decade after independence, the socialist state seemed to some of Burma's leaders to be further away. The truth is that the socialist approach only partially solved the main problems of the Burmese economy. The foreigner became less and less important in the economic direction of the country, and rice exports increased (Burma exports more rice than any other nation), but not to prewar levels. However, Burma did not make much of a start toward industrialization, nor did she restore mineral and timber production to anything resembling the levels of the colonial 1930's. A decade after independence, almost all capital equipment and many comparatively simple consumer goods, including various food items, had to be imported.

The results of the first decade of socialism have been similar in Indonesia. There has always been a strong socialist bias to Indonesian nationalism, but there has not been the strong ideological commitment that there was in Burma. The major wave of nationalization of Dutch companies and estates in primarily agricultural Indonesia, for example, did not come until the second half of the 1950's, in contrast to Burma's immediate takeover of most of the biggest British holdings. (Even then, it was done in retaliation for Dutch retention of Indonesian-claimed western New Guinea.)

The Indonesians engaged in development planning from the

start, but they concentrated at first on small-scale and cottage industries. Their concern with larger projects dates only from 1953. The Indonesians were plagued with less immediately threatening obstacles than Burma, yet socialism so far has not appreciably modernized the Indonesian economy; nor has the standard of living been raised. However, the government has been successful in its efforts to boost rice production (although not to the point of self-sufficiency), and at least a start has been made in the direction of industrialization.

Indonesia's lack of success has not deterred President Sukarno, who seems personally more of a socialist now than he was in the early 1950's. He offers a sharp contrast to Burma's U Nu, who has drastically watered down his socialism in terms of immediate goals. Burma seems to draw one conclusion from its socialist experiences, Indonesia quite another.

The third socialist state in Southeast Asia—more socialist in intent than experience—is Singapore. The socialism of the ruling People's Action Party is extremely leftist in character, though it is not Communist. However, Singapore became self-governing only in mid-1959, and the PAP has been much more cautious in its actual economic policies than its earlier pronouncements suggested it would be—largely because it has not wanted to frighten the conservative government of adjacent Malaya, with which Singapore would like to merge. Nevertheless, the PAP leadership will probably continue to stress the rapid industrial development of the once British colony of Singapore, which must import most of its food requirements. The full range of the PAP's socialism has not yet been applied and may not be until the question of Singapore's future relationship with Malaya is resolved one way or the other. Rubber-milling and tin-smelting, Singapore's main industries, are both declining.

The Philippines and Malaya have not been characterized by a socialist orientation toward the economic organization of society. Both countries have employed various devices associated with socialism, such as state planning, but their economies are basically private in character, and their present leadership seeks to keep them that way. Some government-run enterprises exist in the two lands, there are controls, and the states have sought in various ways to stimulate development of particular aspects of the economies. But they have done no more in this direction than practically every other twentieth-century capitalist nation does.

There are several reasons why Burma and Indonesia inclined toward socialism and the Philippines and Malaya did not. Significantly, these two pairs of countries obtained their independence from foreign rule under quite different circumstances. Although the British granted Burma her freedom from colonial rule in 1948 without a fight, Burmese nationalism had been building up for nearly half a century, and the British did not tell the Burmese until 1947 that they would set them free. Indonesia, of course, fought four hard years to get its independence from the Netherlands. On the other hand, the United States capitulated early to Filipino nationalist demands and ultimately set up a timetable for independence, while the British consciously nurtured a Malayan national sentiment after World War II and cooperated to the maximum extent with those who led the country to freedom. In short, the Philippines and Malaya did not experience frustrating years of bitter struggle against Western colonial rule, nor was there the tendency in these lands to think of the imperial government or Western businessmen as capitalist exploiters.

In all four countries, there were private elements able and willing to assume the responsibilities of economic leadership. But in Burma and Indonesia, nationalist resentment was directed as much against these private interests—which happened to be Chinese and Indian—as against the colonials. The Philippines, although not without its own commercially able Chinese, also possessed indigenous businessmen in numbers and experience without parallel in either Burma or Indonesia.

Both the Philippines and Malaya, moreover, received considerable assistance from the United States and Britain, respectively, to restore their disrupted economies following World War II (an advantage not enjoyed by the Burmese or the Indonesians) —which made the task of running their own economies after independence less staggering. And their more cordial relations with their former colonial rulers provided assurance of any further necessary economic help. In short, socialism was not the only alternative.

Of the two countries, the Philippines has been less inclined toward large-scale government participation in the economy; in fact, the leaders view the government's role in the national economy in even more restricted terms than does the nation's onetime colonial ruler, the United States. The Philippine economy is primarily agricultural; coconuts, sugar cane, and abaca account for more than three-fourths of all shipments from the Islands. During the colonial period, Filipino goods entered the American market duty-free, as did U.S. products in the Philippines. Independence changed this economic relationship, a change for which the Philippines was not prepared. The 1946 Bell Trade Act, however, since modified, provided for a gradual reduction (beginning in 1954) in tariff preferences until their complete disappearance by 1974, when, it had been hoped, the Philippines would be able to stand on its own two feet economically. But the nation has made only limited progress in this direction, partly because the government, as the result of opposition from the major agricultural interests and unimaginative leadership, has not fully used its powers for the purpose of reorienting the economy.

The Philippines' main agricultural crops remain in private hands, and despite widespread dissatisfaction over concentration of land ownership, there is no likelihood of any early governmental takeover. A land-redistribution program exists—the enabling legislation having been passed during the Magsaysay period—but it is a weak one and has not been effectively implemented. Magsaysay was able, however, to improve the terms of the tenant's relationship with the owner of the land he worked and to increase the government's supervisory responsibilities in this area. The government also has used its control over foreign exchange to influence private-investment policy, but it has not been as effective in this as it might have been. It has been more successful in its efforts to encourage the development of manufacturing enterprises through financial assistance from the Industrial Development Center and other means.

Malaya's economy is also predominated by the private sector, but the Malayan Government has used its economic powers more imaginatively than have the Philippine leaders. Rubber and tin are the kingpins of the Malayan economy. British interests still dominate both fields, and they are followed in importance by the country's resident Chinese. The Malays play practically no significant role in the national economic life, despite the fact that they (together with the racially related Indonesian migrants) constitute half the population. As indicated by its announced plans for the 1960-65 period, the Alliance Government is seeking to give the Malays new economic importance in their country through development projects in the principal areas where they live. The hope is that this will help correct economic inequalities between the Malays and Chinese and lend new political stability to the nation.

Malaya's moderate leadership desires continued growth of the private sector of the economy, including new investment from abroad, but realizes that there are economic tasks to which private capital is not attracted. It is in the latter area that the government has concentrated its economic efforts—not for the purpose of establishing a socialist state, but to develop the economy as rapidly and as soundly as possible, as well as to equalize the roles played in it by the various racial communities. The government has also given private investors economic help in certain areas such as rubber replanting. The purpose of the Rural and Industrial Development Authority is both to promote economic development and to assist the rural population to improve its living conditions.

The other countries of Southeast Asia, with the conspicuous exception of North Vietnam, follow economic policies that are less subject to clear-cut classification than those of Burma, Indonesia, Singapore, the Philippines, and Malaya. This is partly because the leaders either have not really thought through their intentions in this area of state policy (as in the case of Thailand) or have been too busy with other problems (as has South Vietnam).

North Vietnam has quite definite ideas about the uses to which government should be put in the economic field—adopted largely from the example of neighboring Communist China—and has sought to implement these. Ho Chi-minh's economic policies were organized long before the partition of 1954 created the two Vietnams. Agrarian reforms redistributing the land and lowering land and interest rates were begun by the Vietminh in the territory it ruled during the period of the civil war against the French, although the war did interfere with implementation of the program. After the 1954 Geneva settlement, the Communist Government of North Vietnam stepped up the pace of its reforms, classifying its subjects as landlords, rich peasants, middle peasants, poor peasants, and landless peasants, and proceeded to redistribute the land to the last two groups at the expense of the first two. Even more important, the North Vietnamese Government has made a serious effort to industrialize its half of the divided country, largely with help from other Communist states. By the beginning of the 1960's, private industrial investment was almost nonexistent. North Vietnam's economy remains predominantly agricultural, but it is changing; industrial products accounted for 18 per cent of the total value of output in 1939 (under the French), and 29 per cent in 1959 (under the Communists).

Neither South Vietnam nor Laos has really made a commitment concerning government's role in the economy. The economies of both countries have relied heavily on foreign assistance, which so far has come mainly from the United States. The government has played its most important role—and it has been a questionable one in Laos—in the disposition of such aid. South Vietnam has absorbed more than 900,000 refugees from the Communist north, settling most of them in various agricultural projects. In 1957, President Ngo Dinh Diem announced a five-year plan of limited proportions, but its details were never published—nor was the plan implemented. Economic activity in South Vietnam is conducted primarily by private interests, although the government has sought to make sure that these interests are Vietnamese—to the extent of declaring, in 1956, that all Chinese born in the country were Vietnamese citizens, whether they wanted to be or not (and many of them did not).

Laos has had only limited opportunity for the development of economic policies, although critics of past conservative governments claim that the nation would have had less political troubles if more had been done in the economic field. The country is one of the most underdeveloped in the world (it has no railroads at all), and its economy is almost exclusively based on self-sufficient peasant agriculture. Actually, Laos is neither socialist nor capitalist, but, more accurately, pre-capitalist (or pre-modern). Government has been used in only a very limited way in the economic field—despite the establishment in 1956 of a National Planning and Foreign Aid Council for preparation of a five-year plan. Communist Pathet Lao support among the rural peasantry partly reflects this. The Communists promise greater governmental economic activity, but, whoever ultimately wins out politically in Laos, the burden of economic development will be a heavy one.

Marshal Sarit Thanarat has made greater efforts to develop Thailand economically than his predecessors; the Six-Year Plan, which came into force in January, 1961, was in fact the country's first. The revolution of 1932, in which Pridi Phanomyong was a leading civilian participant, lacked genuine economic objectives. Pridi himself, however, was interested in the Thai economy and advanced certain psuedo-Communist proposals that almost ended his career as a major political figure. The economic policies of Premier Phibun Songkhram, who came to power in the late 1930's, were more nationalist than socialist. Phibun, who had to leave office because of his cooperation with Japan, returned to the premiership in 1948 and resumed his prewar economic policies, with resulting widespread corruption and unplanned development. Since Marshal Sarit's second coup, in 1958, Thai economic-development policy seems to be better coordinated. The emphasis is now on diversification and industrialization, although the economy remains basically agricultural, with rice the most important product and export. The government is by no means neglecting the rice sector of its economy; its seed-improvement program, for example, is being aimed at development of a better-quality grain.

Thailand's government is an important participant in the commercial and industrial life of the country and will probably become even more active. At the same time, though, there is a vigorous private sector that the government seeks to supplement rather than supplant; indeed, the export of rice, previously a state monopoly, was opened to private businessmen in 1955. There appears to be no ideological reason for the particular approach of the Thai Government; development, as such, seems to be its main goal. Neither in objective nor in result can Thailand's economic policies yet be considered socialist.

Socialist goals have been espoused by Prince Norodom Sihanouk's People's Social Community Party in Cambodia, where one of the main problems in terms of economic development is that there is comparatively little private business to help carry what is a very great burden. And much of this private business is controlled by aliens, mostly Chinese, Vietnamese and Frenchmen. Despite Prince Sihanouk's apparent socialist orientation, Cambodia's inclination toward an active role for government in the economy seems to be motivated more by reasons of expediency than ideology. A limited start has been made toward industrialization, including the assembly of a small French automobile to be exported to Communist China. The economy remains basically agricultural, however, with rice and rubber the principal crops.

### Social Welfare

The attitude in Southeast Asia toward government's role in social welfare varies from country to country, as do intentions and capabilities to implement social policies.

Since Burma's socialism is based partly on humanitarian considerations, it is not surprising that the country's leaders have concerned themselves with working conditions, health problems, and the welfare of the young and the old. They have proclaimed many policies in these areas, but have implemented far fewer. Housing units, for example, built under the government of Premier U Nu, had to be rented for sums beyond the means of those for whom they were originally intended. Maternity benefits provided by law cover comparatively few women and are claimed by even fewer. It is not that Burma's leaders have not tried. The main difficulty lies in the country's inadequate resources to finance advanced social-welfare policies.

Malaya did not begin its independent existence with a socialist motivation for welfare activity, but it has enacted much social legislation and put most of it into practice. Malaya's governmental leadership is at the same time interracial and pro-Malay, and this is reflected in its social-welfare policies. Those most in need of assistance are the less fortunate Malays, and the government has sought to help them. The Malayans have also expanded social services developed by the British and inaugurated activities in other areas; for example, schools and hospitals have increased in number considerably in the few years since independence.

The social-welfare outlook of the reigning People's Action Party has prompted Singapore's government to initiate several new projects, such as low-cost urban housing and reclamation of neglected rural areas. Singapore's problem—and the problem of all the governments in the area—is whether it will be able to support twentieth-century social-welfare activity with its limited economic resources.

Despite its revolutions and generally rough-and-tumble politics, Thailand has also steadily increased its social services. Neither innovations of the new independence nor the continuation of programs begun by the colonial ruler, these services have been developed by the Thai themselves over a long period, taking as their model Western activity in various fields. Each of the country's 71 provinces (or states) today has at least one government hospital, while social-security coverage includes old-age and disability assistance, maternity and child-welfare care, and other benefits. Laws also have been passed that control workers' hours, wages, and conditions. Many Thai are not covered by some of this legislation, but coverage is being steadily expanded.

The government in Indonesia has made progress in the social-welfare field, but the dimensions of the problems in Southeast Asia's largest country dwarf the accomplishments. Indonesia began its independent existence with grandiose promises from Sukarno and others of the things the government would do for the population now that the exploiting Dutch had departed. Although major advances have been registered in some fields— education and health, for example—the government has merely passed laws in other areas without implementing them. Preoccupation with the struggle for political power, the country's shaky economic position, and the shortage of trained personnel partially explain the limited social progress. President Sukarno still tells the people what he intends to do for them, but he now meets a measure of cynicism among large segments of the population.

A good many of the promises that have been made have been kept in North Vietnam. Ho Chi-minh and his political comrades, although as imaginative as Communists elsewhere in propagandizing their subjects, have also expressed concern for the people's needs in the social-welfare field and have done something about them. The stated objective of the government is to provide the social services associated with the more developed Communist countries. There is no reason to doubt that the Communists have every intention of fulfilling this promise—if only to create a showcase of accomplishments.

The record of South Vietnamese President Ngo Dinh Diem's government in this area—as in economic development—is probably not as good as it might have been without the ever-present Communist threat. The government has shown a high sense of social responsibility in some fields, however, such as the resettlement of the refugees from the north. The attempt to improve the living conditions of the peasantry through development of new rural cooperatives, or *agrovilles*, shows what the government can do and apparently has an increasing mind to do. The *agrovilles*, however, are primarily designed to provide community defense against Communist and other terrorists. There is, of course, a relationship between the government's social policies and the Communist threat. Failure to register progress on the social as well as economic front would give a major boost to the Communist cause.

The Philippine Government provides many social services (more than some of its neighbors), but these seem relatively modest in number and scope in view of the political stability of the country, the Islands' resources, and the tradition of such services begun under American rule. Laws exist for the protection of laborers, rehabilitation of the physically disabled is accepted as a public responsibility, and there are 80 government hospitals and some 500 municipal maternity and charity clinics—but many social-welfare projects have failed to get off paper, and there is heavy reliance on various types of organized private-welfare activity. Private hospitals outnumber government ones by more than three to one, and most large private business firms have insurance and retirement programs for their employees. Only government employees have a form of social security.

The achievements of Cambodia in the social-welfare field have been limited, and Laos' past conservative rulers showed practically no interest in this area of public policy.

## Education

There is one problem that almost all the Southeast Asian countries have approached with relative vigor: the education of their youth. They regard this as an area for major use of the resources of government.

Indonesia, which has faced setbacks in other fields, has achieved impressive results in its efforts to expand the educational facilities available to its youth. In 1939-40, little more than 2 million children attended primary schools in the then Dutch colony, and only about 26,500 went to secondary schools. In 1956, almost 7.5 million children were attending primary schools, and more than 636,000 were enrolled in secondary schools. Ten times as many students were enrolled in universities as had been during the earlier period cited.

The results of this educational expansion have been heartening: Indonesians in general are now more literate and informed than at any time in their history. And the national language, which only began to gain acceptance throughout the archipelago after independence, is now widely spoken. But there are also problems. Those who receive an education expect to be able to use it; unfortunately, employment opportunities have been insufficient in independent Indonesia. Moreover, the standard of education has dropped—an inevitable consequence of the tremendous expansion in the number of people being taught.

The experiences of other Southeast Asian lands have been

comparable to those of Indonesia, although in no other country has the educational expansion been as great. The number of young persons attending school in Burma—where more than 1.5 million pupils attend primary schools and nearly 257,000 students are enrolled in state secondary educational institutions—is up, but so is the illiteracy rate, now higher than before the war (probably higher, too, than the official figures indicate). And the drop in educational standards has been greater than in Indonesia. Burma's problems stem partly from Japan's interruption of the normal educational processes during the period from 1942 to 1945.

Education under the British in Malaya was largely a private matter. The Chinese ran their own schools; missionary schools provided probably the best education; and the government met the full cost only for Malay children. The Alliance Government, however, passed legislation in 1957 providing for a national educational system in the form of a six-year primary education in Malay, Chinese, or Tamil, with English a required subject in a common curriculum. Different types of secondary education were established by the same law. Nearly 1.1 million pupils today attend primary schools in Malaya, and more than 120,000 students are enrolled in secondary schools.

The number of children attending school in the Philippines, which probably had the best educational facilities in all Southeast Asia when it was under U.S. rule, has also grown since independence. More than 3.9 million students today attend public schools, and another 810,000 are enrolled in private institutions. Public-school standards have declined, however, and there has been an increase in the diploma-mill type of private school, but the Filipino educational system still ranks as the best in the area. Approximately one-third of the national budget is spent on education (as contrasted with 9 per cent in Burma).

Thailand's school system also is good, partly because, never having been under colonial rule, the Thai have maintained uninterrupted control over education in their country. More than 3.5 million students attend the country's more than 21,000 elementary and secondary schools (which increased in number by over 1,600 in 1959 alone). Communist North Vietnam has made impressive and probably justified claims of educational advances; more than 650,000 pupils attended primary and secondary schools in 1959, and 2.2 million participated in adult-education classes. South Vietnam has given major attention to the problem and also made genuine progress, with public expenditure for education increasing nearly 29 per cent between 1958 and 1959. Expansion of educational facilities rates high among the priorities of the government of Singapore, which has been critical of the character of past English-style education; total enrollment today is in excess of 290,000 students, but less than half the schools are government-operated ones. There has been advancement in Cambodia, too, but the country's limited resources, both human and economic, pose a major obstacle. Laos has accomplished more in education than in other areas, but the results are still of modest proportions. Nearly 375,000 pupils attend primary schools in Cambodia, but only slightly more than 12,000 are enrolled in secondary institutions. In Laos more than 77,000 students go to public primary schools, and less than 2,000 to secondary ones.

### National Unity

National unity is singularly important because failure to attain it can prevent achievement of other objectives. This is why all the governments of Southeast Asia have used various powers, including that of persuasion, to try to pull their loosely integrated nations together into more cohesive units.

In the first years of independence, Burma faced rebellions instigated by two brands of internal Communists, the left wing of the Peoples Volunteer Organization, and a variety of ethnic minorities (Karens, Mons, Arakanese Mujahids, and Shans). In addition, the presence of large Indian (700,000) and Chinese (350,000) minorities posed other difficulties relating to national unity. Burma responded to this complex problem in various ways. Premier U Nu fortunately enjoyed the confidence of most of the leaders of the minorities, and this made some peaceful progress possible. Military action was taken against those in revolt, although amnesty offers also were repeatedly made. The Karens were given a state within the semifederal Union of Burma, and the Mons and Arakanese were promised states if it could be determined that their people really wanted them. State support of Buddhism also drew Buddhists of the different races closer together, but Christian Karens, Moslems, and Catholics, among others, were disturbed by U Nu's promise in the 1960 election campaign to make the majority's faith the official religion of the land.

Indonesia's dissidents at varying times have included, among others, the Communists (who staged an abortive coup in 1948), discontented soldiers (such as the followers of Colonel Zulkifli Lubis, who tried to assassinate President Sukarno in 1957), the fanatic Dar-ul Islam insurrectionists (who seek a theocratic state), and those who staged the ill-fated Sumatran and Celebes revolt of 1958-61. Sukarno, unlike Nu, tends to repress rather than conciliate dissatisfied elements—including those who have *not* rebelled against the government.

The problem in Malaya is basically different than in Burma or Indonesia. The Malayan constitution accorded the indigenous Malays a preferred position because the country was traditionally theirs and they clearly required such an advantage to hold their own against the Chinese in the first years of independence. The Chinese political elite, or most of them, have accepted this— though understandably, without much enthusiasm. The Alliance leadership has so far kept racial differences from increasing or assuming violent form, but this is something very different from real national integration, which still seems to be a thing of the future.

Burma, Indonesia, and Malaya have each clearly taken different approaches to the problem of national unity. The Malayans have followed a policy of integration, the Indonesians a more repressive policy, and the Burmese something of both. All three countries, however, have recognized the need for governmental action, as, indeed, have all the countries of the region. Thailand, the Philippines, and South Vietnam have followed both restrictive and integrative policies toward their large Chinese minorities, while the Cambodian Government has checked the commercial activities of its Vietnamese and Chinese minorities. The challenge to national unity in Laos has come not from any particular ethnic group but from the externally supported Communist Pathet Lao movement, although the Pathets have skillfully exploited the animosity of the minority hill tribes against the majority lowland Lao. The fighting that broke out anew in the country in 1960 stemmed largely from resumed efforts to suppress the Communists.

The problem of divided Vietnam is also clearly one of national unity, and both regimes have utilized the resources of government, including force, to retain the loyalty of their subjects.

## Law and Order

The problem of national unity in South Vietnam, as in some of the other countries of the region, is closely related to the task of preserving law and order, a basic function of government. Ngo Dinh Diem faced a very serious problem when he assumed the premiership (the office of president did not then exist) in 1954. Contrary to the Geneva settlement, large numbers of Communist cadres had been left behind by the Vietminh in the wake of partition, and there were three private organizations in the country with their own armies: the Binh Xuyen gangsters, the allegedly Buddhist reformist Hoa Hao sect, and the syncretist religious movement known as the Cao Dai. Each of these groups sought to stake out an area for itself free from the control of Diem. The Binh Xuyen and Hoa Hao armies were eventually defeated, and the Cao Dai backed off from a head-on encounter.

For a while, steady progress was made against the internal Communist threat, but cadres of the Communist Viet Cong were never quite rooted out. These cadres, dominating many villages, and armed bands, some of them coming from North Vietnam, challenged the government increasingly during 1959-61. "The government now controls only the big cities," wrote an on-the-spot observer at the time of the November, 1960, coup attempted against Diem; "insecurity begins only ten miles from Saigon."* According to official American estimates, about 600 persons were

* Sal Tas, "The Revolt in Vietnam," *The New Leader,* XLIII (November 28, 1960), 4.

killed each month in skirmishes involving Communists in the first half of 1961—a much higher casualty rate than in the French-Algerian war. South Vietnam obviously is still faced with a major internal-security problem.

Burma, Malaya, Laos, Indonesia, and the Philippines have all had major internal-security difficulties, too, while Thailand, North Vietnam, Cambodia and Singapore have been more fortunate in this respect. The problem of law and order in Laos has centered mainly on the three-cornered political struggle for power among the conservatives, neutralists, and Communists. Already in possession of the two northeastern provinces of the country at the time of the 1954 Geneva settlement ending the Indochinese war, the Communists were integrated into the national administration following the 1957 Vientiane Agreement and then lost their two cabinet portfolios in a shift of political strength to the right. Both before and after serving in the government, they fought against it. During these periods, effective law and order did not exist in large areas of the country. Military force was used against the Communists almost continuously—but without any success. The victories of the Pathet Lao rebels and their neutralist allies over the conservative central government in the first half of 1961 indicated the likelihood of continued disturbances in the country—whatever the character of any temporary settlement among the disputants. The prospect for early political peace seemed limited—except within the framework of some kind of Communist-dominated state.

As indicated previously, Burma's internal-security troubles began in earnest literally weeks after the start of independence. By mid-1949, the government of Premier U Nu controlled only the capital city of Rangoon. No sooner had the government begun to turn the tide of victory than remnants of Chinese Nationalist forces that had fled from the Communists joined with various insurgent elements. Moreover, some Burmese took to the bush simply for the purpose of banditry. The worst of the difficulties were over by the mid-1950's, but even in the early 1960's the security situation, though better than at any time since British rule, still left much to be desired—with frequent banditry, continued Karen insurgent activity, and a revolt by some Shans.

The government in Indonesia has never been as seriously threatened as the Burmese regime was in 1949, but the country has had at least one rebellion in progress throughout the post-Dutch period, and there are bandits of the sort that plague Burma. For twelve years (1948-60), Malaya was faced with an externally inspired Communist revolt, in which mostly Chinese segments of the populace participated. The insurrectionist Hukbalahaps, remnants of which still exist in eastern and southern Luzon, posed a serious problem for the government in the Philippines between 1947 and 1952.

### Development of a Military Establishment

With the exception of perhaps North and South Vietnam and Thailand, disturbed security conditions have been the single most important factor in the creation of larger and more important armies in Southeast Asia. The 150,000-man South Vietnamese Army was built up, with American assistance, to meet the possibility of invasion—by one means or another—from the Communists to the north. The North Vietnamese Army of 350,000 men is ostensibly "defensive," but presumably would exploit any situation to the south.

Thailand's military services—army, navy, air force, and national police—have grown steadily in the three decades since the revolution of 1932. A fairly proficient small military force existed before then and, in fact, supplied some of the participants in the revolt. Under Phibun Songkhram, who was Premier during the periods 1938-44 and 1948-57, the various military arms grew to be the most important organized groups in the country, a position they retain today under Field Marshal Sarit Thanarat. The Thai services, estimated to number today between 90,000 and 100,000 men, perform both internal and external security duties for the state.

The Burmese Army was created specifically to quell the rebellions that followed independence. Nationalist leader Aung San formed a fairly formidable military force under the Japanese, but this was partly disbanded after the war when it became apparent that freedom from British rule would be obtained.

Defections from the small Burmese Army in the first years of rebellion made a major effort necessary to put together an effective fighting force to combat the rebels. This was done—and done well—by General Ne Win, the army's commander-in-chief, and by Premier U Nu. The result is today's army of some 100,000 well-trained, experienced men.

The army in Indonesia has largely been used for the same purpose as in Burma: the preservation and restoration of internal security. Born of the revolutionary fight against the Dutch, Indonesia's military forces (the army, navy, and air-force components of which total approximately 250,000 men) are comparatively well trained and have stood up reasonably well under the stresses and strains of postcolonial politics. The army, indeed, is almost absolutely necessary for the survival of Indonesia at the present time. Without it, there might not be a single Indonesian state today.

The Laotian Army, for the greater part of the period after 1954, at least tried to serve a similar function—but with the very important difference that the military in Laos was less united. The conflict that flared in the last months of 1960 as a result of the August coup led by paratrooper Captain Kong Le stemmed in part from the fact that the 25,000-man army had split over the question of whether to cooperate with or suppress the Communists. However, the independent Laos of the early 1960's owed its existence to the army, which—like the armies of South Vietnam, Thailand, Burma, and Indonesia—was the single most important group in the country. The army split of 1960 was more of a splintering than a division of the army into anything resembling equal factions, but this was enough to eliminate the role of the military as a force for stability in the country. The weight of numbers seemed to be on the side of the anti-Communist military leaders, but this was not sufficient to assure government successes against the rebels in the fighting during the first months of 1961. An army that is not willing to fight is hardly an effective army—and the military forces of the government in the civil war of 1961 lacked the apparent drive and sense of purpose of their adversary.

In the three other independent countries of Southeast Asia—

Malaya, the Philippines, and Cambodia—the army is not yet as important an institution. The Malayan Army, the youngest in the area, is by no means a prop of the regime. The 50,000-man Philippine armed forces played an important role in defeating the Communist Huk rebels, but it regards its primary role as international in character—i.e., the fulfillment of Philippine treaty commitments under the SEATO alliance and under the bilateral defense arrangements with the United States. Cambodia's defense establishment, which numbers 35,000 men, apparently sees itself as guardian of the country from invasions by Thailand and South Vietnam—which the highly sensitive Prince Sihanouk seems to fear.

The development of a military force for security purposes is a recognized function of government. But some of Southeast Asia's armies, not content with their security duties, have encroached on other areas. The army dominates all phases of national life in Thailand, where the military has had the longest time to develop. The situation in Burma is progressively becoming similar: The Burmese Army today runs the country's biggest department store, catches and sells fish, breeds poultry, and imports and sells automobiles. The creation of strong military establishments to help maintain law and order and defend the realm has clearly produced a problem of its own: control of the military. It is a problem that probably will grow before it diminishes.

\*  \*  \*

The uses of government in Southeast Asia vary for several reasons, ranging from the ideological orientation and personalities of the leaders to the different legacies of the former colonial rulers. The variation is greatest in the approach toward organization of the economy and least pronounced in educational programs. The leaders of some of these countries have inclined more toward greater utilization of government in the years since independence, while others have grown more cautious or conservative. Everywhere, however, government is big government in the sense that it dwarfs the other social institutions. There are no exceptions—only variations.

SIX

# PERSISTING PROBLEMS—
# AND SOME CHANGING POLICIES

THERE HAVE been important changes in the environment in which
public policy is formulated in most Southeast Asian countries
since the first days of independence. Naturally, various policies
have changed, too. But others, surprisingly, have not changed—
and are not changing.

The decade of the 1960's shows evidence of being appreciably
different from the previous decade in many ways. For one thing,
some leaders have modified their thinking about what can be
done in the short run to develop and modernize their national
economies. And problems have been identified that were previously not recognized, while common sense appears to have
joined ideology and grandiose aspirations as one of the important
influences on policy formation. In short, a considerably more
knowledgeable and experienced leadership directs some of these
lands today.

Furthermore, the first period of disintegrative tendencies has
been weathered sufficiently well to inspire hope that most of
these countries will be able to hold themselves together under
the strains of the 1960's. For example, the internal Communist
threat in most cases is not the immediate challenge to the survival of the state that it was in the late 1940's and early 1950's—
the most conspicuous exception being civil-war–torn Laos.

Things are looking up—in some places.

## Economic Policies

The country that seems to have made the biggest policy adjustment in the economic field is Burma. Surprisingly, perhaps, it was not basically because of the change in economic tactics that the country's top political leadership split in 1958. This clash was primarily one of personalities, involving the ambitions and fears of Deputy Premiers U Kyaw Nyein and Thakin Tin; the latter was joined by Premier U Nu for private rather than policy reasons. The split, which divided the country politically, produced in its wake a major internal-security problem, which was one of the main reasons for the army takeover of September-October, 1958.

The primacy of the internal-security problem was recognized by the country's leaders the year before they split. Nu announced publicly in June, 1957, that Burma's inexperienced leaders had erred in embarking upon ambitious economic-development and social-welfare plans before assuring the existence of the minimum conditions of law and order necessary for the success of such plans. He admitted that there had been bad planning, limited numbers of trained personnel, and insufficient financial resources.

Nu also announced before the split that the country had made at least two other major policy errors: It had placed too much emphasis on industrialization at the expense of development and diversification of basic agriculture, and it had not made sufficient use of the capital resources of private businessmen, both Burmese and foreign. Nu's pronouncement seems to have been accepted by his two chief lieutenants, Deputy Premiers U Kyaw Nyein and U Ba Swe. Moreover, his views had support in the army, as illustrated by the economic policies followed by his successor, Premier General Ne Win.

The Ne Win Government, during its eighteen months in office (October, 1958, to April, 1960) stimulated the change in emphasis of Burmese economic policy. Rice sales abroad, previously monopolized by the notoriously inefficient State Agricultural Marketing Board, were opened to private businessmen, and other state monopolies were ended. The army-operated Defense Services Institute, probably the single most important economic group in the country, entered into joint-venture arrangements with foreign firms and governments in several areas and took on a variety of new functions, including shipping and the import of coal. (The previous Nu administration had inaugurated the joint-venture approach, which has proved very popular in Burma as elsewhere in Southeast Asia.) Cultivators were encouraged with bigger payments for the higher-quality rice that was developed with the government's help. No new industrial activity was inaugurated during this period; some manufacturing enterprises were curtailed, and others were the objects of efforts by the army leadership to make them more efficient. Planning continued to dominate the Burmese economic approach, though, and Brigadier Aung Gyi, once a leading socialist politician, became the economic czar of the land.

Many of the Ne Win reforms were innovations only in the sense that they were being pushed more vigorously than previously. General Ne Win and his chief lieutenants were certainly not antisocialist. And U Nu, who returned to office in April, 1960, has continued along the socialist path. There has actually been no change in basic economic direction, merely a change in the pace at which the Burmese move toward the goal of a socialist state. Burma's leaders have recognized that conditions beyond their control preclude the country's moving as rapidly toward this objective as had been expected in the first years of independence.

Another kind of change has taken place in the Philippines. The Philippine political leadership, basically conservative in economic outlook, has been forced by circumstances to direct the government toward a greater role in economic activity. In 1956, the participation of the government in gross fixed capital formation was 25 per cent, as contrasted with twice that figure in the case of Burma. However, the Five-Year Plan issued by the National Economic Council of the Philippines in 1957 called for an increase in the percentage of government investment to 40 per cent. The Philippine economic outlook remains free-enterprise–oriented (in the American sense), but a modification of official thinking concerning the government's role in the economy was discernible in the latter half of the 1950's. The necessity of state planning was recognized almost from the start by the Filipino leadership, but it was an extremely modest version of government planning by the general standards of former colonial lands—and it was not effectively implemented.

Interestingly enough, the Philippine Five-Year Plan placed increased emphasis on the industrialization of the country, which is just the opposite of what Burma's Premier Nu did in his major address on economic policy in the same year. Unlike Burma's young and ideologically motivated socialists, the leaders of the Philippine Government probably had attempted much less than could or should have been done to industrialize the country during the first decade of independence. The government is now seeking to develop those areas of the national economy to which private capital is not particularly attracted, and it seems more aware of how it can use the resources of the state in the economic field than it did in the early years of independence. The Filipino leadership has always felt that there were some areas of economic activity where direct government participation was more expeditious than private enterprise, but the change in emphasis is no less significant for this reason.

There is a need for at least a tactical change in economic policy in Indonesia also, but the Indonesian leadership has shown only limited recognition of this fact. President Sukarno has always been socialist-oriented, and he has become much more so in recent years. Some of his opponents even go so far as to call his present-day socialism pseudo-Communism. But Sukarno has his own name for it: "guided economy." And, as in the case of guided democracy, he intends to do the guiding. A major economic objective of his guided economy has been, and is, the confiscation and nationalization of all Dutch and Chinese properties, and eventually of all private enterprise. The Indonesian leader apparently is not shaken by the addition of new economic responsibilities to the already overburdened shoulders of the state. Sukarno confiscated various Dutch interests in the latter half of the 1950's, when Indonesia's economic problems were of such dimensions that all financial and managerial resources available, including those of the Dutch, were needed. Experience is not always the best teacher.

The new eight-year development plan, which was proclaimed in August, 1960, and went into effect in January, 1961, is ambitious in the grand Sukarno manner. Providing for the construction of more than 850 projects, it aims for an increase in Indonesia's national income of 236 billion rupiahs, or 11.7 per cent, by 1969. The cost, according to the government, will be 240 billion rupiahs ($5.3 billion, at the official rate of exchange). The ambitious development program calls for a yearly investment rate of approximately 13 per cent of Indonesia's current national income and earmarks 45 per cent of the total expenditure for investments in means of production.\*

Many Indonesians are highly skeptical of even approaching the plan's lofty goals. It is far too ambitious, some claim, while others question some of the assumptions, particularly financial ones, on which it is based. Such misgivings are reasonable, and it would not be unfair to regard the new program as akin to the big promises of the past that were rarely kept.

Yet, there is in the 1961-68 development plan, and in President Sukarno's remarks about it, at least a hint of new thinking. The emphasis of the plan is clearly on diversification and expansion of production, which is a healthy change from the previous concern with the task of dividing up an undersized economic pie rather than making a bigger one. Sukarno himself showed refreshing caution when he warned against expecting too much too soon from the plan, predicting, among other things, that it would take another quarter-century for all the homes in Indonesia to have electricity. Though his outlook has probably not changed basically, this could signal the beginning of a change.

The objectives of Cambodia's first five-year plan (1960-64), called the Norodom Sihanouk Plan, are modest by Indonesian standards, despite the fact that it calls for an annual increase of 3 per cent per capita in the national income. Primarily concerned with agriculture, stock breeding and rearing, and forestry and fishing, the plan envisages some industrialization, but this will be of modest proportions and will involve mainly the processing of local raw materials. According to Cambodian expectations, for-

\* See dispatches by Bernard Kalb, in *The New York Times*, January 2 and 10, 1961.

eign aid would finance the plan to the extent of 42 per cent in the first year, dropping to 20 per cent in the fifth. The Norodom Sihanouk Plan—which followed the "preparatory" 1957-58 two-year plan and a 1959 one-year complementary plan—was officially expected to bring only "partial improvements in the nation's economy" and no more than "a slight rise in the people's standard of living."* The change (if it can be called that) in Cambodian economic policy has been in the direction of more socialism as in Indonesia, rather than less state economic activity as in Burma.

The economic activities of President Ngo Dinh Diem's government in neighboring South Vietnam, on the other hand, have always been modest. During the first years of its independent existence (after the 1954 Geneva partition), South Vietnam probably used government in the economic field less than any of the other major countries of Southeast Asia. However, the late 1950's saw the beginning of a change. South Vietnam has not yet embarked on any major industrial-development program, but it is seeking to diversify and develop its resources, which up to now have been limited basically to two crops, rice and rubber. It greatly increased rice production to an exportable surplus of 350,000 tons in 1960. And a major land-reform program, inaugurated in 1957, had resulted in the transfer of more than a million acres to new owners by 1960. Progress clearly is being registered, and the government is assuming greater responsibilities, although not on the scale of the socialist countries. There has, however, been a small amount of government-encouraged industrial expansion in recent years—and the National Investment Fund and the Industrial Center are institutions that may be used more vigorously in the future to encourage more rapid development.

Governmental economic responsibilities are on the increase in Malaya; and so is private investment, both foreign and domestic. The development program for 1960-65 (1 billion Malayan dollars†) calls for expanded government developmental activity. If

* "The First Five-Year Plan for Cambodia," *Cambodia News* (Washington: Royal Embassy of Cambodia), IV (January 31, 1961).

† Three Malayan dollars are worth one American dollar.

this program is implemented as well as past Alliance intentions have been, it should raise the country's per capita income, now second only to oil-rich Brunei in Asia, even higher. In addition to encouragement of industrialization, the government also has proposed land developments, costing more than $105 million, to assist rice-growers over the next ten years, and it plans to spend an additional $10 million on a new rubber promotion program under which smallholders would receive $100 an acre for planting rubber on previously jungle land.

Both governmental and private economic activity are also on the increase in Thailand. A Board of Investment was established in 1959 to stimulate private investment, and the pattern of industrial ownership in the country is becoming increasingly one of joint participation by the Thai Government and foreign investors —a pattern that also characterizes most of the other Southeast Asian lands. The Industrial Promotion Act suggests that future industrialization will favor the private sector and will concentrate more on medium- and large-scale manufacturing enterprises. A new loan authority, the Industrial Finance Corporation, began operations in late 1959.

Like Malaya, its neighbor to the north, Singapore is a state on the move. It has to be, for its population and Malaya's are the fastest-growing in Southeast Asia today. More than half of Singapore's inhabitants are under twenty years of age. Some of these are already looking for jobs, and others will be in just a few years: Upwards of one-fifth of the total working-age population are today unemployed or significantly underemployed.

The traditional economy of Singapore was that of an entrepôt, but Malaya's independence and the economic nationalism of other countries like Indonesia and Thailand, for which Singapore formerly performed transshipping and processing functions, are forcing adjustments. Singapore would like a common-market arrangement with Malaya, but Malaya's lack of enthusiasm for this and broader merger proposals has been so obvious that Singapore's ruling People's Action Party has gone ahead with its own five-year plan, which anticipates the expenditure of 1 billion Malayan dollars and duplicates some of Malaya's development activity. With or without Malaya, the socialist PAP sees

Singapore's survival as a prosperous economic unit primarily in terms of industrialization. A hard-working population and the availability of capital are among its assets. But Singapore is an island of only 225 square miles, and it lacks the raw materials for significant industrialization. Without economic progress, however, extreme leftist elements in the PAP and the island's Chinese majority could force a turn toward the U.S.S.R. or Communist China for economic and other help.

This, of course, is already the orientation of North Vietnam. Since the partition of 1954, North Vietnam has gone through many of the same stages as China did during its first decade under Communism, although Chinese-style communization has not yet begun. Peking Radio announced in 1961, however, that 85 per cent of North Vietnam's peasant households had joined producers' cooperatives by the end of 1960. Increased collectivization of agriculture as a means of stimulating food production was a major aim of the three-year agrarian program announced in 1958—which could be a prelude to the establishment of Chinese-style communes. Meanwhile, industrialization proceeds in North Vietnam, as evidenced by the construction of a 100,000-ton steel mill at Thai Nguyen. Of all the countries in Southeast Asia, North Vietnam is probably the most diversified in terms of its mineral resources, which include coal and iron. The hydroelectric-power potential of the country is also considerable. Both the Soviets and Chinese have given major assistance to North Vietnam's state-directed industrialization program, and increasingly impressive results may be expected.

## Future Economic Development

Burma, which has recognized that it cannot pull off a socialist and industrial revolution overnight, should register slow progress during the 1960's and then enter into a period of more rapid economic development. Socialism and industrialization remain major Burmese goals. They may be modified even further, but they probably will not be abandoned. The Burmese may be expected to step up their efforts on behalf of better rice and more of it, as well as agricultural diversification, but not as an alternative to modernization of the economy.

The Philippines, despite its basic free-enterprise orientation may be expected to move in the direction of greater and more direct governmental participation in the economy. The Philippine approach will probably increasingly resemble that of Malaya.

The private and public economic sectors of Malaya and Thailand already seem to have made a satisfactory accommodation and should be able to further adjust to the demands of the future as their economies become more modernized. Malaya's chief dilemma will probably continue to be the economic role of its Malaysian population. If the government persists in its present policy of vigorously encouraging the Malays to assume economic roles in the society, it will sooner or later presumably start pre-empting areas into which Chinese capital and personnel might have moved. This could produce a troublesome situation, but the only apparent alternative to such a policy is perpetuation of the current plural economic society, which hardly provides a solid base for a democratic national political unit. The problem would be complicated if there were any sort of union between Malaya and Singapore—and this is the major reason why there is not likely to be one. But the Malayan Government seems to be aware of how dangerous a frustrated Singapore would be—to Malaya as well as to Southeast Asia as a whole—and presumably will cooperate with its nearby island neighbor, if only to the minimum extent necessary.

Actually, Malaya is strongly disposed toward economic and other kinds of cooperation with all its Southeast Asian neighbors. Prime Minister Tengku Abdul Rahman, together with President Carlos P. García of the Philippines, has proposed an Association of Southeast Asian States. The ASAS would not be a political or military alliance along the lines of SEATO (the U.S.-backed Southeast Asian defense treaty alliance), but a means of economic collaboration among the countries of this area, as well as a device for encouraging greater cooperation in general among them (including closer cultural ties). One of the possible ways in which the ASAS might express itself, Prime Minister Rahman has suggested, would be a common market among the Southeast Asian lands. Another (and related) objective might be the development of a program of regional specialization wherein wasteful duplication would be eliminated, with the various countries developing their national economies in some kind of coordinated manner. Malaya's Premier and the Filipino and Thai foreign ministers agreed at a February, 1961, meeting to establish a joint working group to study opportunities for mutual benefit with which the ASAS might concern itself. Other nations have generally responded favorably to the ASAS proposal, but Indonesia in particular, the largest in the region, has not.

Indonesia's reaction to ASAS is typical of its tendency to think of itself as a more important nation than any of its Southeast Asian neighbors. The host to the Bandung Afro-Asian Conference of 1955 appears to regard itself more as a member of the Asian community than as a part of Southeast Asia. Moreover, Sukarno has not demonstrated any eagerness to change his course or to go along with the suggestions of others. Inflexible in a manner unlike either socialist-oriented Burma or the free-enterprise– inclined Philippines, Indonesia has not bent with the wind of circumstances. Undoubtedly, it will have to in time—unless its leadership can manage indefinitely to bail the country out with foreign economic aid. Socialism and industrialization, however, will continue to be the goal, even if Indonesia takes a cue from the Burmese example of retrenchment.

The problem of South Vietnam is different from that of any other Southeast Asian land. The South Vietnamese cannot afford Indonesia's kind of economic stagnation, even in the short run. The government of President Ngo Dinh Diem, or a successor regime, must get the country's economy on the move in order to survive. The ever-present example of adjacent Communist North Vietnam requires matching accomplishments. Nearby Cambodia, too, will probably be influenced by Ho Chi-minh's state. Whether the result will be reaction or imitation cannot be predicted. On the other hand, even more underdeveloped Laos, another of North Vietnam's neighbors, appears destined to remain in its present backward state for a long time to come—regardless of who rules it.

North Vietnam may be expected to continue its economic growth, particularly its industrialization. In fact, Ho Chi-minh's government may economically outstrip South Vietnam to the point where even the most determined efforts by the Diem regime would not enable it to catch up with its Communist rival.

The cost of such Communist progress will probably be high in both economic and noneconomic terms. Many Southeast Asians, extremely critical of regimentation, will not fail to realize this. At least one free Southeast Asian country, Malaya, is also off and running in terms of economic development. It should serve as an attractive countermodel. In addition, diminutive but vital Singapore has the human and technical resources for rapid growth, and Thailand's recent economic advancement is impressive. The Philippines and even Burma could make much more economic progress in the 1960's than in the previous decade. So could Indonesia, richest of all the countries of the region, if it could only get its political house in order.

The main models of economic development, however, will probably not be North Vietnam, Malaya, or any other Southeast Asian state, but India and Communist China. Indian failures presumably would not seriously affect those lands which are themselves enjoying modest success, but Indian economic successes could encourage greater effort and courage on the part of the non-Communist countries of Southeast Asia. The shortcomings that are even now apparent in the economic policies of China are not missed by many Southeast Asian leaders. For the Chinese example to have maximum impact upon Southeast Asia short of conquest or the establishment of indigenous Communist governments, China's triumphs would have to be coupled with both a conspicuous lack of success on India's part and failures by the Southeast Asian countries in their own development efforts—an unlikely combination of events in the near future.

### Social Welfare

The problem of retrenchment in social-welfare programs is more difficult than changing the emphasis of economic policies. The beneficiaries of such social services object to having them modified, even if the benefits involved are only on paper. Yet, however strong the case for governmental social services, these are costly burdens for economies such as those of Indonesia, Burma, or South Vietnam. A shorter work week may be desirable in Detroit, Hamburg, or Marseilles, but not necessarily in Djakarta or Rangoon at this time. Nations that should be tightening their belts have been seeking to enjoy the benefits of enlightened twentieth-century social legislation. But the Southeast Asian nations are not twentieth-century countries economically.

Certain social-welfare policies appear to be necessary in any society. Child-labor laws and various types of medical care, for instance, may now be more imperative in such countries as Malaya or the Philippines than in the United States or the United Kingdom. The problem—and it is a big one—is how to support a medical-care program with an underdeveloped economy.

Some of the present governmental social services are not only costly but wasteful in their manner of operation. Incompetent and inefficient direction, not to mention corruption, have taken their toll. Thus, one possible method of retrenchment, with only limited political consequences, would be to overhaul current operations to make sure they are accomplishing their goals at the lowest cost. This would not be enough, however, for a major reduction of the burden, leaving as the lonely alternative that foreign governments, private organizations, and/or the United Nations pick up at least part of the bill. Such aid would have to be on a scale greater than that of present-day technical assistance—both bilateral and U.N.—because the more necessary kind of social policies remain paper ones in most of the area.

Government-provided social services are likely to expand—with or without outside help. Singapore's ruling People's Action Party is particularly keen on enlarging government's role in this sphere. Radical elements that threaten to subvert the PAP Government and the continuing potential attraction of Peking for its Chinese leave Singapore no choice but to maintain its policy of expanded social services. South Vietnam, possibly even more than Singapore, faces the challenge of doing enough for its people to outweigh the attractiveness of Communism for them. Malaya and Thailand (which have more of the means to finance such programs) are almost sure to increase their social services, while the comparatively well-off Philippines probably should be doing more in the social-welfare field than it is.

Burma's leaders probably will not substantially expand social services in the near future, since they still remember the chaos caused by their overextension on the economic and social front in the first decade of independence. However, Premier U Nu is a quite unpredictable person and can be easily swayed in terms of the welfare of his people. President Sukarno undoubtedly will promise the Indonesians more, but it is difficult to see how he will keep such promises in view of the country's shaky economy. North Vietnam will probably make further progress, which no doubt will be widely heralded; but the progress will be only as much as is deemed necessary, in view of the heavy demands of economic development upon the resources of the state.

### Education

The increase in the number of students attending school in Southeast Asian countries is impressive, but the quality of the education they receive is not. Educational policy must shift its emphasis from quantity to quality if it is to fulfill its high purposes.

Burma provides an excellent example of the consequences of sacrificing quality for quantity. The Burmese Government, in its all-out egalitarianism, made university education free to anyone meeting certain minimal qualifications, instead of controlling quality as well as quantity by charging for such education and providing scholarships for needy students of ability. The government has permitted students to retake examinations they had failed. This has not only lowered the quality of education, but resulted in overcrowding of facilities. The level of university instruction is also inadequate. Some lecturers read notes copied from their British teachers during the colonial years of the 1930's. There are outstanding teachers, of course, but not many. And student discipline is at times practically nonexistent.

The quality of lower-school education compares even less favorably with more developed countries. Teachers are poorly rained in most instances and insufficiently paid in all. The examination system leaves much to be desired. The private schools are he best in the country, but these are run mostly by missionaries, nd obstacles are placed in their way by the government.

An appreciable early rise in educational standards is unlikely n either Cambodia or Laos. But Malaya, Singapore, the Philipines, and Thailand appear to be aware of the need to lift the quality of education. Burma, South Vietnam, and Indonesia do ot seem to recognize as much the necessity for a change, and tandards will probably continue to drop in these lands. The kind, ather than quality, of education is the problem in Communist North Vietnam.

The importance of educational progress cannot be minimized. ncreased literacy and a rise in the general level of education are ecessary for economic development; they also are essential for he early evolution of meaningful political democracy. Equally mportant, education in the national language can play a major ole in linking the diverse peoples who comprise the population f some Southeast Asian countries—a fact recognized particularly y the governments of Indonesia, Burma, and Malaya.

## National Unity

The most formidable resistance to integration in Southeast Asian countries comes not from the government or even the leading representatives of the ethnic communities, but from the lowest conomic, educational, and social levels of society.

Malaya is a particularly good example. The main barriers to national integration in that country are the ingrained attitudes nd social habits of the ordinary Malays, Chinese, and Indians. The Moslem religion and related customs, including dietary laws, have prevented Malay intermarriage with the Chinese thus far nd will probably continue to do so. Informal residential segregation, however, is being partly broken down by public housing, nd an increasing number of Chinese are learning the Malay anguage, removing an important cultural barrier.

The Chinese pose only one of Burma's minority problems, although an important one in view of the long common border with China. Burma also has an Indian minority, which is twice as large as the Chinese element. And there is still the task of integrating such indigenous peoples as the Karens, Shans, Kachins, Chins, Arakanese, and Mons. The worst of the ethnic group opposition to what has been called the "Burmanization" of the country seems over, but some fresh trouble is probable. Present efforts to establish Buddhism as the state religion are also causing discontent. The economic position of the minority Indians, who are to Burma what the Chinese are to the rest of Southeast Asia, will probably deteriorate, Burmese racial feeling being what it is. Nevertheless, geographical considerations and the size and prominence of the Burman majority make an increasingly unified nation likely in the long run.

Resident Chinese minorities pose major problems of national unity for Thailand, Indonesia, South Vietnam, the Philippines, and Cambodia. Intervention of one sort or another by Communist China is a possible consequence if the governments of these countries fail to integrate the Chinese into their respective societies. This task is more difficult for Indonesia, a Moslem nation, than for Thailand, the Philippines, or Burma, where there has already been much intermarriage. Even in these three lands, however, the Chinese remain essentially a group apart from the rest of the population, partly as a result of government policies.

The obstacles to national unity in South Vietnam and Laos result, more than anything else, from the efforts of the Communists to divide the people. A major program of assistance to the rural populace might have been one way for past conservative Laotian governments to reduce some of the countryside support for the insurgent Pathet Lao, but this was not forthcoming—thus paving the way for the setbacks suffered by the anti-Communists at the hands of the Pathet Lao during 1960-61. Nor is there any indication that South Vietnam is about to become the kind of showcase for democracy that its rival to the north is bidding to be for Communism. Indeed, partly for this reason, South Vietnam could become another Laos in terms of increasing Communist guerrilla activity, feeding on the dissatisfaction with the existing administration.

## Law and Order

Continued disturbed conditions of law and order are likely in South Vietnam, while Laos seems destined for either a Communist political takeover or, should pro-Western elements show new strength, renewed civil strife (international "neutralization" notwithstanding). The Laotian conservatives lost the internal struggle for power in 1960-61—though the country was not immediately lost to outright Communist domination. The worsening domestic security situation in South Vietnam in 1960-61 also showed clearly that President Diem had by no means ended the Communist danger to his strategically situated land. Without outside help, South Vietnam or Laos could again become the scene of full-scale civil war—with all that would mean in terms of misery for their people and political setback for the West in the Cold War. Cambodia, another non-Communist country that used to be part of French Indochina, has not been seriously troubled in the manner of either Laos or Vietnam, but Communist successes against its two neighbors could mark it as the next trouble spot in Southeast Asia.

The current Laotian situation suggests that repression, although an important factor in checking internal disturbances, Communist or otherwise, is not enough. It is unlikely, however, that this is fully appreciated yet in South Vietnam, which still has a chance to escape Communist domination. It probably is not appreciated in North Vietnam either, but Chinese overlordship precludes any but abortive revolutionary activity there.

Disturbed internal conditions are least likely in the next few years in the Philippines, Malaya, and Thailand—although the increase in Communist strength in Laos will afford greater opportunity for external efforts to stir up trouble in Thailand. Indonesia's internal-security prospects, however, are dim. A change in President Sukarno's attitude toward those dissatisfied with his rule could reduce the possibility of future rebellion, but such a change seems unlikely. The army probably holds the key to Sukarno's continuation in power, and it is also the main check against internal disorders of a nonpolitical character. The army is also the chief hope for internal peace in Burma.

**The Role of the Army**

The maintenance—or restoration—of satisfactory conditions of internal security in most of the Southeast Asian countries has required the development and employment of an army, and this has produced a problem of its own. The Burmese coup of 1958 and the Laotian seizures of power in January and August, 1960, show that soldiers are not willing to remain in the background when the civilians let the situation get out of hand or pursue policies with which the military leaders are in disagreement. The problem stems basically from the need for a strong defense force and the inability of the civilian leadership to control the soldiers. The lack of a tradition of civilian supremacy and the increasing importance of the military organizations in this part of the world add to the difficulties.

Once an army has been created and developed, there are obvious obstacles to reducing its proportions or prominence. Burma's U Nu knows this as well as anybody. Nu, together with the army's commander-in-chief, General Ne Win, worked to build an effective military establishment to fight the Communists, Karens, Chinese Nationalist irregulars, and other armed elements, but the army he helped to create subsequently dislodged him from the premiership. Having returned to office, Nu undoubtedly will seek to remain on good general terms with the army leadership, but he may also attempt to win friends for himself within the ranks of the military and to shift more of the responsibility for internal peace to the national police. The latter is a sensible policy anyway, but it must be followed cautiously in order not to damage army morale or give rise to another coup.

Like armies elsewhere in Southeast Asia, Indonesia's has exacted a price for its services and has distinguished itself in the ancient governmental art of empire-building. It has not infiltrated every activity, but it has not done badly for itself. Part of the cost of the army's continued support of President Sukarno unquestionably will be his backing of its further expansion. Presumably, this is a price Sukarno is willing to pay to stay in office. However, it raises a major question about the long-term role of the military in Indonesian life.

Failure to answer this question adequately in Laos contributed to a split in the ranks of the military in 1960 that was exploited by the Communists. Laos had a serious enough burden on its hands with its Communist Pathet Lao troubles, but the problem developed new and more serious proportions when the army stopped being an arm of the government and tried to be the government. The political importance of expressed Communist concern for the plight of the rural peasantry and exploitation of anti-Lao sentiment among the hill people notwithstanding, it was the superior skill and spirit of the Soviet-supplied Pathet Lao rebels and their "neutralist" military allies that determined the outcome of the struggle for power in the country in 1960-61. It is highly unlikely that any Laotian settlement—be it neutralization, partition, or coalition government—will end the importance of soldiers, guerrilla or otherwise, on the rugged Laotian political scene.

The abortive effort of a faction of the South Vietnamese Army to oust President Diem in November, 1960, fits into the same pattern. Unless Diem modifies some of his policies, the attempt will probably be made again. If he does make changes, the army will have obtained at least part of its objectives.

The problem of control of the military is by no means new in Southeast Asia. Thailand has been grappling with it unsuccessfully for more than a quarter-century. The Philippines, Malaya, Singapore, Cambodia, and North Vietnam are unlikely to go the way of Thailand in the foreseeable future, but other neighboring countries might. Control of the military is—and will continue to be—a major problem of public policy in most of the Southeast Asian countries for some time to come.

*       *       *

The greatest changes in public policies of the Southeast Asian countries have taken place in the economic sphere. Failure to control their growing armies could bring a change in policy toward the military—that is, if the soldiers have not grown too powerful to veto any such moves. Lack of resources might also necessitate curtailment, or a reduction in the rate of expansion, of the social services provided by the various governments.

Changes or not, however, the problems of the region stubbornly remain: economic development, social welfare (including education), national unity, law and order, and the role of the military. If these problems are not solved, whatever the policies or the forms of government, there are those who will seek to exploit the resulting dissatisfaction. Foremost among these, of course, are the Communists, who are old hands at the game.

# Seven

# THE COMMUNIST CHALLENGE

THE DECADE and a half following World War II was characterized by an ebb and flow of the immediate Communist threat to the nations of Southeast Asia. The 1954 partition of Vietnam, with the Communist Ho Chi-minh gaining control of the northern half of the country, was the major development of the period in the persisting Communist conspiracy, but these years also saw serious Communist-led revolts in Burma, Malaya, and the Philippines; an abortive Communist uprising in Indonesia; and Communist-encouraged protracted political instability in Laos. The Laotian problem assumed major-crisis proportions in 1960-61 and caused widespread concern as the possible starting point for a larger conflagration. If the Communist challenge seemed to have developed overnight, it came as no surprise to the one-time colonial rulers of Southeast Asia. It had plagued them in colonial days, too, although not so much as in the first years of the new nations' independence.

### Before World War II

The first Communists in Southeast Asia set foot in the then Dutch East Indies in advance of the 1917 Bolshevik Revolution in Russia. They were Dutch Marxists who had founded a party in 1914 called the Social Democratic Association. Their arrival in the Indies followed by only five years the first organizational stirrings of Indonesian nationalism. Sneevliet, the most important of the Dutch Communists, was expelled by the colonial government in 1918, but not before he had laid the groundwork effectively. He left appropriately indoctrinated Indonesians to carry on his work.

These Indonesians associated themselves with the Comintern in 1920, when the Indonesian Communist Party as such—today the country's oldest continuously functioning political party—was formed. Before this time, however (and subsequently), the Communists made bids for control of Sarekat Islam, Indonesia's first mass nationalist organization. Falling short of success, they were read out of the party in 1922.

Communism, seeking to exploit nationalist antipathy for the Netherlanders, posed probably the single most important political problem facing the ruling colonial Dutch during the 1920's. The Communists sought again and again to capture control of the nationalist movement, and, failing this, some of them revolted against the colonial government in late 1926 and early 1927. The revolt was quickly subdued. It was an impetuous and ill-timed action, taken without the support of the Comintern. The Communists had previously successfully organized important sectors of Indonesian labor, but these and other gains were offset by the folly of the abortive revolutionary attempt.

Communism was subsequently declared illegal, most of the leading Communists were arrested and expelled, and many non-Communist nationalists were also detained (even though the Dutch knew they had not been involved in the uprising). The Communists regrouped themselves and began to grow again in the 1930's, but they did not again become the threat they had been in the 1920's.

The first Communists in Indonesia were Dutchmen who were not agents of the Russian Bolsheviks, but the Soviet Union soon recognized the opportunities for exploitation of the discontent in the colony. For Lenin, the objective was a "revolutionary union of the progressive countries" with "the revolutionary masses of the oppressed in all colonies and all Oriental states." Indonesia was the largest colonial holding in Southeast Asia, and a revolutionary situation was already developing there, so Indonesia received high priority in the Communist conspiratorial design against Southeast Asia.

The groundwork for what was to be Southeast Asia's first Communist government was also laid during this period. The leader of the Communist movement in Indochina then, as after World War II, was Ho Chi-minh, first known as Nguyen Ai Quoc. Born about the same time as Chiang Kai-shek, he shipped to Europe as a kitchen hand when he was fifteen, arriving in time for World War I and the Russian Revolution. Ho became acquainted with Communist thought in France, wrote spiritedly on the subject of Vietnamese independence, and became a founding member of the French Communist Party in 1920. The youthful Vietnamese Communist then went to the U.S.S.R. and subsequently to China, where he served as nominal translator-assistant to Michael Borodin, Soviet adviser to Chiang Kai-shek. Ho fled China in 1927 in the wake of the split between the Kuomintang and the Communists, but not before he had founded the Revolutionary Youth Fraternity of Vietnam.

Three years later, Ho organized the Indochinese Communist Party at a meeting in Hong Kong, bringing together previously opposed revolutionary groups. Ho's party was founded a decade after the Indonesian Communist Party, but it shared with its comrades in the Dutch East Indies the benefit of considerable ideological spadework prior to its institutional formalization. The Indochinese Party, despite its name, focused its attention almost exclusively on Vietnam. Cambodia and Laos were then of minor concern to it. The Communists (labeled the "Red terror" in the wake of the 1930 Yenbay Mutiny) were a major object of the colonial administration's counteractive "white terror" and were almost wiped out. The orthodox Communists did not play an important role in Indochina for the remainder of the 1930's, although a Trotskyite party, based in the south, was a factor in continued nationalist agitation. Ho Chi-minh, who had also been a Comintern agent with responsibilities beyond Indochina, disappeared. He did not assume an important role again until 1941, when he emerged as a founder of the Viet Nam Doc Lap Dong Minh Hoi, or Vietminh (Vietnam Independence League).

The only other country in which the Communists were a major force before World War II was Malaya, where they were then, as later, largely Chinese in personnel and orientation. What became the Malayan Communist Party began as the left wing of the overseas Chinese Kuomintang (or Nationalist) Party in Malaya and Singapore. The overseas Chinese were a source of financial support for Sun Yat-sen and the Chinese revolution of 1911. The Kuomintang and later the Communists remembered this precedent. The Kuomintang had established itself in Malaya by the early 1920's and had an active left-wing (or pro-Communist) faction by at least the middle of the decade that infiltrated labor unions and schools.

When the Kuomintang and the Communists split in China in 1927, the inevitable repercussions were felt in Malaya. The necessary response of the Communist Chinese in Malaya was to form a new political organization. This was not difficult because of the various bodies they had already set up, such as the South Seas General Labor Union. In 1928, accordingly, they established the South Seas Communist Party, a name that accurately indicated a wider area of activity than merely Malaya and Singapore. The Chinese refer to Southeast Asia as Nan Yang (the South Seas), and the Party, reflecting its name, had branches for all other lands in the area except the Philippines.

The South Seas Communist Party changed its name to the Malayan Communist Party a couple of years later and reduced its area of operations as a result of the founding of Ho Chi-minh's Indochinese Communist Party. Still another organizational shake-up followed almost immediately when a French Comintern agent, Serge Lefranc, was apprehended in Singapore in 1930. Lefranc revealed the intercountry Communist network existing in this part of the world. His information led to the arrest by the British of the Vietnamese Communist leader, Ho Chi-minh, in Hong Kong.

Subsequently, in the 1930's, the Malayan Communist Party became the most active of all the parties in Southeast Asia. This was partly because its Chinese character afforded it the opportunity to exploit the anti-Japanese sentiment of the most vigorous of Malaya's several ethnic communities. Infiltration and strikes were the main activities of the Party before the "united front" period of world Communism in the late 1930's. In general, these were years of growth—and successful ones—for the Malayan Com-

munists, but they were never able to overcome their chief lia-
bility (at the same time an asset in appealing to the Chinese as
such): the nonparticipation of Malaya's other races in the Party.

The only other country in which Communism apparently was
predominantly Chinese in character was Thailand. The absence
of foreign political control, the general satisfaction of most Thai,
and the lack of a political orientation among those outside the
ruling elite created an environment without nourishment for Communism. There was, however, a Communist Party in Thailand
during these years, founded by at least 1929, and a few Thai
were associated with it. But it was so insignificant, its activities
were so covert, and its numbers were so few that hardly anything is known about it even today.

Burma, like Thailand, was characterized by only limited Communist activity in the 1920's and 1930's. The Burmese Communist
Party, founded only in 1939, was the last to be established in the
various colonies of Southeast Asia. The South Seas Communist
Party sought to undertake the formation of a party in Burma in
the late 1920's, but was not successful. Communism as an ideology, however—especially in its explanation of colonialism as an
inevitable result of the weaknesses of capitalism—was attractive
to many students and other young leaders in the 1930's. The Party
as such was an outgrowth of Communist intellectual inroads
among certain students, with direct encouragement for its establishment coming from India's Communists—hardly surprising in
view of the fact that Burma was a province of India until 1937.

Communism in the American-governed Philippines, as in Thailand, lacked its usual number-one whipping boy: a colonial power
that gave no sign of departing. The Philippines had been
promised independence almost from the start of the association
with the United States, and the final step in this direction, which
was to culminate in national freedom in 1944, was taken in 1934.
The Philippine Communist Party, officially launched in 1930, had
to seek other conditions to exploit, and these it found in the discontent of the tenant farmers of the country. The Party was forced
underground a year after its official inauguration, however, following its designation as an illegal association. The pseudo-
Communist Socialist Party, undoubtedly assisted by the Com-

munists, took up the cause of the dissatisfied peasantry. The Communists were again legalized in 1938 and in the same year merged with the Socialists, retaining the title of Communist Party. Although neither the original Communists nor the Socialists— nor the merged Party formed in 1938—represented a serious rival at the polls to the popular nationalist patriot Manuel Quezon, the extreme left wing did steadily increase its support among the rural masses of the country. The ground was laid for what was to be the Philippines' single most important internal political problem after independence, the Hukbalahap revolt.

### The Japanese Interlude

World War II changed the context of politics drastically in Southeast Asia, and the Communists sought, with varying degrees of effectiveness, to capitalize on this change. By early 1942, Japan ruled all Southeast Asia. In every country—except noncolonial Thailand, which was an ally (willing or otherwise) of Japan— the Communists played a major role in nationalist resistance movements. They usually either joined with other groups in opposing the Japanese or, if the activities were not coordinated, fought the Japanese simultaneously. In two countries, however, the Communists were the only resistance force—with important consequences for the postwar years. One of these countries was Vietnam, the other Malaya.

The Vietminh, launched by Ho Chi-minh in China in 1941, carried the brunt of the resistance against the Japanese, to whose rule the French had reluctantly acquiesced. The Chinese, who were justifiably suspicious of Ho's intentions, created a second nationalist coalition movement, the Vietnam Revolutionary League, but this never proved to be a serious rival for the Vietminh. The latter, as the war years progressed, developed an extremely effective military arm, which numbered some 10,000 men by 1945. Before the war ended, the Vietminh was the de facto government of rural Tonkin, which comprises the greater part of today's North Vietnam. The rallying cry of the Vietminh was nationalism, not Communism, and this, coupled with its entrenched position in the northern part of the country, served it well after the war.

The Malayan Communists also almost singlehandedly carried the burden of resistance against the Japanese. But they did not have the advantage of a strongly held territorial base of control or of widespread support from the population as a whole. Many Chinese did not support the Communists, whose army was known as the Malayan People's Anti-Japanese Army, and the Party was completely lacking in Malay backing. The monopoly of the wartime resistance, in short, did not serve Communism's objectives in Malaya as well as it did in Vietnam. Nationalism was already a potent force in Vietnam, and the Communists captured control of it, but there was as yet no nationalism in Malaya. Moreover, Malaya's Communists were highly suspect among the Malays because they were Chinese.

In Burma and Indonesia, the Communists and non-Communist nationalists cooperated in the struggle against the Japanese. The Communists at first were the main force in the resistance movement in Burma, but there were others. In 1944, practically all the nationalist groups, Communist and non-Communist alike, were brought together in the omnibus Anti-Fascist People's Freedom League. However, some of the nationalists also cooperated with the Japanese, while maintaining contact with and protecting their colleagues in the underground. This happened in Indonesia, too. Nationalists Sukarno and Mohammed Hatta, later President and Vice President of the Republic of Indonesia, worked with the Japanese—on behalf of their people—while the socialists Soetan Sjahrir and Amir Sjarifuddin (later revealed as a Communist) directed main arms of the underground resistance movement. In the Philippines, Communists and non-Communists alike opposed the Japanese, although many non-Communists also cooperated with them. The two wings of the underground failed to cooperate with one another and actually fought among themselves. One was American-directed, the other Communist in its leadership; the latter, the People's Anti-Japanese Liberation Army, formed the nucleus of the postwar Hukbalahap movement. The resistance movement in Thailand, known as the Free Thai Movement, was directed by Premier Phibun Songkhram's longtime political rival,

Pridi Phanomyong. It was pro-American and more leftist probably than Phibun and his pro-Japan clique, but it was by no means Communist.

### Communism in Indochina

The wartime years helped to set the stage for the kind of Communist activity that followed the victory of the Allies over Japan. Only in one Southeast Asian country, however, did the Communists move quickly to take advantage of the situation. This was Indochina—or, more narrowly, Vietnam, where the real struggle took place. Japan had granted independence to the Vietnamese (and to the Cambodians and Lao) in the spring of 1945, and the Vietminh, capitalizing on its monopoly of power in the country, induced Emperor Bao Dai to abdicate and proclaim an independent republic with Ho Chi-minh as its president and Bao Dai himself as supreme political adviser. The republic was declared on September 2, 1945, before the French returned.

France's return to Indochina was delayed because of its occupied status during the war, and it was the British and Nationalist Chinese who took over from the Japanese, north and south (respectively) of the sixteenth parallel. When the French did return, they were unwilling to compromise with the Vietminh or other nationalists. However, France did formally recognize Ho Chi-minh's "Democratic Republic of Vietnam" as a "free state, having its own government, parliament, army, and treasury, belonging to the Indochinese Federation and the French Union" in an accord signed on March 6, 1946, but various French officials subsequently sought to sabotage the agreement. In late 1946, French bombardment of the Vietnamese section of the city of Haiphong, killing more than 6,000 persons, resulted in Vietminh retaliatory action. Thus was launched the eight-year Franco-Vietnamese, Communist-nationalist war.

The war went steadily against the French, primarily because the preponderance of popular support lay with the Vietminh. The movement led by Ho Chi-minh had succeeded in identifying itself with the cause of nationalist resentment against foreign rule. One reason why it was not too difficult for the Vietminh to merge Communism and nationalism was the fact that Ho himself was both a nationalist and a Communist, much like Yugoslavia's Marshal Tito. The French, denying facts that could not be denied, failed to cooperate genuinely even with nationalists of non-Communist orientation. The task was a tremendous one anyway, Ho's national prestige being what it was, but French policy gave the Vietnamese no alternative that would satisfy the growing nationalist urge for freedom.

Increased assistance from China, following the conclusion of the Korean War, gave the Vietminh a growing capability to hold off the French militarily. Then, under the able leadership of Vo Nguyen Giap, the rebels slapped the colonial regime with a series of military setbacks, including the much-publicized fall of Dien Bien Phu in May, 1954. American financial assistance, averaging $500 million annually, was not enough to swing the balance. The outcome was the Geneva settlement of July, 1954, which partitioned Vietnam and gave the Communists control of the northern sector. Elections to unify the country were to have been held in 1956, but these were opposed by South Vietnam's President Diem, who does not believe that free voting is possible in the north. So ended the first wave of the Communist assault in Vietnam; the second wave (discussed in detail later) is now in progress.

Communism in the other two former French Indochinese possessions, Laos and Cambodia, is a postwar phenomenon. It is not yet even a force of major consequence in Cambodia. Laos, however, as the 1960's began, was embroiled in such Communist-encouraged turmoil that its survival as an independent state was at stake.

Under the Japanese in World War II, Laos was given nominal independence. Its small political elite opposed re-establishment of French domination following Japan's defeat. Some sought to oust the French under non-Communist leadership, while others turned for help to Ho Chi-minh's Vietminh in neighboring Vietnam. The Pathet Lao received its indoctrination and its principal support, starting in the late colonial years, from the Vietnamese Communists. Formed from remnants of the Lao Issara (Free

Laos) movement that sought to prevent restoration of French control immediately after the war, the Pathet Lao is led by Prince Souvannavong, half-brother of former Premier Souvanna Phouma (a leader of the so-called "neutralist" faction in the political troubles of 1960-61). Souvannavong set up a "resistance government" first in Thailand and then in North Vietnam and was able to gain control of Laos' two northeastern provinces before the 1954 Geneva Conference only as a result of Vietminh invasions of Laos in late 1952 and early 1953.

One of the provisions of the Geneva settlement was that the Communists should cease their military activity in Laos and Cambodia. The Pathet Lao held the two northeastern provinces of Laos, however, and despite the armistice agreed upon at Geneva, fighting continued between the Communists and the Laotian Army. Agreement was finally reached in 1957, when the Pathets nominally gave up their provinces, two of their leaders joined the cabinet, and some of their soldiers were integrated into the army. The Communists, forming the Laotian Patriotic Front Party, then concentrated on winning the election of May, 1958, to fill the new seats in an enlarged National Assembly. They did better in the balloting than any of the right-wing parties, and this frightened the conservatives.

The anti-Communists responded by changing governments and removing the Communists from the cabinet. The Communists' countermove was to resume military action, a move facilitated by the fact that a Pathet Lao battalion of 800 men had never been disbanded. A major crisis developed as a result of efforts to contain this group in 1959, with the government charging a North Vietnamese invasion in support of the Pathets. United Nations officials visiting the country found the charge exaggerated. U.N. Secretary-General Dag Hammarskjöld spent a week in Laos and recommended a foreign policy of neutrality: the situation finally calmed down.

The rigged elections of April, 1960, in which the conservatives showed unbelievable strength, set off a chain of events culminating in a neutralist army coup in August. This, in turn, started a three-cornered war in which would-be neutralists, Communists, and right-wing army elements battled one another. Soviet aid to the Pathet Lao and its allies in 1961 made Laos a major crisis that threatened to explode into full-scale war. International negotiations opened in Geneva in May, 1961, to "neutralize" Laos, and a conference among the main political factions began at the same time in Laos itself (at Ban Namone). The United States and the conservative Laotian leaders charged the Pathets with major cease-fire infractions from the start, however—and Communist delaying tactics at both conferences were obvious.

The remaining Indochinese country, Cambodia, has never been invaded by the Communists in the sense that Laos was by Vietminh troops during the Franco-Vietnamese war. It is probably the Southeast Asian country least threatened by internal Communism at present, but it may well have to face such a problem in the near future.

## Postwar Developments in the Other Countries

The 1948 Communist revolts that broke out in three lands—Burma, Malaya, and Indonesia—followed a Communist-sponsored February meeting in Calcutta of the Youth and Students of Southeast Asia Fighting for Freedom and Independence. These insurrections, if not ordered by Moscow, certainly conformed with the new tactical line announced by a major Soviet spokesman at the inaugural meeting of the Cominform in 1947. The Philippine Government also found itself fighting Communist revolutionaries in 1948, but this uprising had begun the previous year.

Burma's Communists emerged from World War II as participants in the coalition Anti-Fascist People's Freedom League. One of the top Communists in the country—Thakin Soe, who had been a resistance fighter from the start while his old friend Than Tun, another Communist, served in the Japanese-installed puppet government—did not like what he regarded as his inferior position in the AFPFL. A dogmatic Communist who called himself a Trotskyite, Soe bitterly opposed any negotiated settlement with the colonial British, and in 1946 he formed his own Communist Party (the "Red Flags"), proclaiming a policy of immediate revolution for independence.

Following the Calcutta meeting, held a month after Burma had obtained its independence, most of the Than Tun–led Stalinist (or "White Flag") Communists also revolted. Thein Pe Myint, one of the original members of the Party in 1939, did not join them; a Communist maverick, he opposed the resort to violence. For a time, in 1949-50, it looked as though the various insurgent factions would topple the government. But Premier U Nu held out courageously, and the Ne Win–led army eventually brought the Communists under control. Meanwhile, the Communists did what the Pathet Lao were later to do in Laos: They formed an aboveground party, the Burma Workers' and Peasants' Party, which, together with other parties, later became the Communist-dominated National Unity Front. The NUF showed surprising strength in the 1956 elections, but the underground Communists remained in the bush. They are still there—what is left of them.

Like their Burmese comrades, Malaya's Communists also switched to armed revolt after the Calcutta meeting. The colonial administration at the time was moving to curb the Party and to dissociate it from the trade-union movement. The Communists adopted a policy of violence in the spring of 1948, and in June the British Government declared a state of emergency. The emergency lasted officially for slightly more than twelve years. It was declared ended by an independent Malayan Government on August 31, 1960. Some 35,000 British soldiers fought against the Communists at the height of the insurrection, which cost the government about $100 million a year. However, the insurgency never posed a real threat to the stability of the government, as it did in Burma.

The Communists' immediate objective did not seem to be the overthrow of the government, although they called for this. They seemed intent on crippling the Malayan economy and weakening the British position in general through the disruption of Malaya's dollar-earning capacity. For a while, the size of the rebel forces remained constant, somewhere around 5,000, despite deaths and captures. Eventually, however, the insurgents were forced to withdraw to the jungle region in the northeastern part of the country adjacent to Thailand, where their numbers steadily dwindled to an estimated 700 men today.

The Philippine revolt, which had already begun by 1948, had

its roots partly in the widespread peasant discontent that produced earlier uprisings under American rule in 1923-24, 1931, and 1935. Six Communists were elected to Congress in the first postwar voting in 1946, but were denied their seats; these included Luis Taruc and Jesus Lava, wartime Hukbalahap resistance leaders. By 1947, these Communists and the Huk movement they dominated, claiming to represent the exploited peasant masses, were in revolt. In 1950, the capital city of Manila was threatened by the Huks, who numbered more than 40,000 armed men. But the imaginative policies of Ramón Magsaysay, who was Defense Secretary at the time, ultimately halted the Huks. They now exist only as a remnant force in southern and eastern Luzon.

The year 1948 also saw Communist-spurred civil war in Indonesia. It started in August at Madiun in eastern Java and was over by the end of October—the shortest insurrection by any kind of revolutionary force during the post-independence period in Southeast Asia. There is reason to question whether international Communism ordered the revolt or whether, like the 1926-27 rebellion, it was an impetuous local affair (which would account for its apparently ill-prepared character). In any case, Communist prestige was damaged considerably, but not so much that the Party was not able to stage a comeback in the ensuing decade. The Communists placed fourth in the 1955 elections to the House of Representatives, receiving slightly more than 16 per cent of the vote in a polling that saw no party win more than 22.3 per cent. The Communists subsequently cooperated with President Sukarno while simultaneously seeking to widen the breach between him and other major political factions.

Communism has been less of an immediate threat in the two other states of Southeast Asia, Thailand and Singapore, but it may be one in the future. There has been no politically important indigenous Communist activity in Thailand in the period since World War II, although there are Communists in the country. Probably the bulk of Thailand's Communists are Chinese. Singapore's Communists also are Chinese, which is a reflection mainly of the predominantly Chinese character of that island state. But there is no overt Communist Party in Singapore because it is banned.

### The Situation Today

At the beginning of the 1960's, Communism was firmly entrenched in North Vietnam. There is no doubt that this state is as much a dependency of Red China as Indochina was of France. North Vietnam is expected to mirror increasingly the pattern of development in China, including Chinese-style communization in time. Moreover, China will probably seek to advance its own position in Asia and the world through use of its southern neighbor. North Vietnam serves the Chinese well as a buffer state, particularly since there are no natural frontiers in this area. North Vietnam also provides Peking with a means of blackmail against the non-Communist nations; it can encourage its satellite to increase pressure on Ngo Dinh Diem's government or move eastward into Laos.

The 1954 Geneva settlement called for the departure of the Communists from South Vietnam. Many did not leave, however, while others subsequently slipped into the country. President Diem is fearlessly anti-Communist, but his government has not rooted out the Communists from South Vietnam. The Viet Cong rebels, whose numbers had been reduced to between 3,000 and 4,000 in 1957, now total something like 9,000 to 12,000. Prior to mid-1956, the North Vietnamese Communists apparently had some hope of unification of the divided country through elections that they could influence by terrorism; but passage of the two-year deadline set by the Geneva agreements and the uncompromising attitude of Diem occasioned a change of tactics. This was when the Communists decided upon a markedly stepped-up assault of violence and sabotage in South Vietnam, although it took until 1959 for the effects of this policy really to be felt. The numbers of the Viet Cong and their strategy of operating in the rural areas to a large extent have caused Diem's 150,000-man army and 50,000-man civil guard to spread their strength. Through 1960, the Communists largely confined themselves to guerrilla raids, terrorization of village populations, assassination of local officials, and sabotage of the government's economic and social-welfare programs. But in early 1961, they grew bolder, taking on the army in pitched battle—generally unsuccessfully.

Aid from the United States in the amount of $1.4 billion (through 1960) has helped Diem's regime to survive, but conditions clearly continue to be precarious.

The situation in Laos is even more bleak. The support of Captain Kong Le's neutralist army faction and Soviet supplies (including armored cars, artillery, and jeeps, as well as small arms) helped the pro-Communist Pathet Lao to gain control over nearly half the country by May, 1961. American aid (most of it military) amounting to $310 million since 1955 seemed unable to help Laos' conservative politicians and soldiers in preventing the Communists from taking the strategically important central Plaines des Jarres in northern Laos, as well as the two northernmost provinces of the country. When the Geneva and Ban Namone conferences began in May, 1961, the Communists and their allies controlled important road junctions and areas where they could land and launch aircraft. There seemed no likelihood that any force, internal or foreign, could get them to relinquish the territory they had already acquired. Their efforts at the Ban Namone conference in Laos to form a coalition government for the entire country apparently stemmed from their desire to extend their influence. The Communists' acquiescence in an at least nominal cease-fire and their willingness to attend both conferences—at a time when they were winning—appeared to parallel 1954 Red tactics at a previous Geneva conference, when the Communists sought legitimization of their de facto political position in North Vietnam through international recognition of the situation. At Geneva and Ban Namone in 1961, the Pathet Lao seemed to be seeking both foreign and internal recognition of the fruits of their recent victories. However, such recognition will no more mean the end of the Communist threat to all of Laos than it has in Vietnam since the 1954 partition agreement for that country.

The immediate Communist threat to Indonesia is not a military one as long as Indonesia's army remains strong and basically anti-Communist. However, the Communists have been gaining ground steadily since 1948 by nonviolent methods. They have no reason to resort to violence—unless the army moves against them, in which case they would not stand much chance of success anyway. The Communists do not now control Indonesia's government; but they are not opposed by that government, as they are in the Philippines, Thailand, Malaya, or Burma. Besides its strength as a party and its influence on President Sukarno, Communism in Indonesia also has a hold on major segments of the labor movement, reputedly has supporters in all the military services, possesses allies (if such they may be called) in the country's pro-Peking Chinese, seems to be increasing its inroads among the students, and is increasingly effective in exploiting economic discontent and disappointment with the results of independence.

The Communist rebellions that broke out in Burma and Malaya in 1948 dragged on for more than a decade. Burma's Communists still remain in revolt against the central government, although their military significance today is very small. In 1959, the Ne Win caretaker administration stated officially that there were only 1,046 White Flag and 338 Red Flag Communist rebels still at large. The pro-Communist National Unity Front, victorious in forty-eight constituencies in 1956, received only 1 per cent of the popular vote in the free elections of February, 1960. However, Communism remains a potent force in Burma, as evidenced by its popularity among politically inclined students at the University of Rangoon.

Malayan Communists, driven into hiding along the Thailand border, no longer posed a threat to the state by 1960. However, unless the country's Chinese are encouraged to identify their interests with those of the state, new Communist difficulties might develop. Communism could also expand among university graduates, whose numbers are growing, unless adequate job opportunities are available in the future.

The Communist Party is outlawed in the Philippines, and it can hardly be regarded as even covertly a significant force in present Filipino politics. However, Communism will remain a potential danger to the Philippine state as long as the unsatisfactory economic conditions of the peasantry persist.

The problem the Philippines faces is very different from the probable form of the future Communist challenge to Thailand. The Thai peasantry is probably the most contented in all Southeast Asia and is unlikely to support Communism. Thailand's

economy, however, is undergoing change, and an urban prole-
tariat is forming. More young men and women are going to the
country's two universities, and they show signs of increasing
resentment against the wealth and conspicuous consumption of
the ruling military clique and their business and bureaucratic
allies.

Singapore, in effect a city-state, is in much the same situation,
having already experienced pressures from the ranks of its intellectuals and industrially employed. On the other hand, the
main Communist threat to Cambodia is likely to come from outside its borders—that is, from North Vietnam or a possibly future
Communist Laos.

### The Appeal of Communism

Part of the appeal of Communism at the present time lies in
the fact that it seems to be the wave of the future. The dramatic
economic advances of the Soviet Union lend credence to the
claims of Communism, which appear to be further substantiated
by the alleged accomplishments of China. Russia has also captured world leadership in rocket and space technology, and this
impresses many people. The U.S.S.R. has steadily increased its
rank as a world power, and China is following in its footsteps.
At the same time, the British and the French have lost status as
great powers, and the United States is on the defensive, even in
the Western Hemisphere, where the Communists have boldly
gained a foothold in Cuba.

Communism is the newer ideology, claiming to be a higher
form of social organization than capitalism, as capitalism was
itself an advance over feudalism. Paradoxically, it seems able to
win the commitment of people to a creed that is basically
prejudicial to their country's recently won national freedom. In
pre-independence times, the attraction of Communism could be
partly explained in terms of its anticolonial character. Many of
those who became Communists during these years accepted the
Marxist-Leninist formula as a means of ousting their imperial
rulers. However, this aspect of Communism's one-time appeal

does not adequately explain the attractiveness of the doctrine for today's Communist leaders and their followers, both of whom exist in larger numbers than ever before.

There is an intellectual appeal to Communism: It does, after all, claim to explain history, and the explanation it offers is not a difficult one to understand. Its analysis of colonialism as an adjunct of capitalism seems to bear out the experiences of Southeast Asians. Communism as an explanation of the past may not satisfy the knowledgeable student of history, but there are few of these in Southeast Asia, even on university faculties. Finally, Communism not only explains the past, but also predicts the future. There is a certain security in knowing what the future holds.

"Importance by association," a variation on the "guilt by association" psychology, is another strong pull of Communism in Southeast Asia. This kind of thinking, though rarely articulated as such, runs something like this: "The Soviet Union is increasingly important in the world of the mid-twentieth century and may be the greatest power some day. The Soviet Union is Communist. I am (or can be) a Communist. All Communists are part of the same world-wide movement. Therefore, I am important because, as a Communist, I share in the achievements of Communism elsewhere in the world."

Among peoples who have been downtrodden for centuries, who were regarded (for the most part) as inferior by the colonial powers, and who find themselves inadequate in many ways to meet the challenges of the new post-European era, the significance of feeling important should not be discounted.

These appeals are, for the most part, psychological, though no less important for this reason. On the other hand, the economic appeal of Communism is also highly significant. All the countries of Southeast Asia are underdeveloped, as Russia was supposed to have been in 1917 and China undeniably was in the twentieth century. Yet, the U.S.S.R. today is a very powerful industrialized nation, and the Communists claim that China is following in its footsteps. If Communism is accepted as the main cause of the Soviet's rapid economic development, then it has an undeniable attraction. Democracy (including socialist-oriented democarcy) is generally slow-moving by nature because it must obtain the consent of the population (or of a majority of it). Under Communism, the leadership can decide and then move swiftly. And speedy solution of economic problems, it is claimed, is what Southeast Asia needs today.

The attractiveness of Communism as a means of rapid economic development, like other aspects of its appeal, is not necessarily related to an individual's own position in the new society. But for some, the pull of Communism is the opportunity for greater personal power or status. This is probably the primary consideration that prompted Burmese Communist leader Thakin Than Tun to resort to rebellion.

Communism's appeal should not be considered only in terms of the leaders who become firmly committed to the creed. In Southeast Asia today, there are also hosts of followers of Communism. The Communists in Indonesia, for example, probably have the broadest popular base of any party in that country. The Vietminh revolt against French rule in Vietnam could never have been the success it was without genuine support among the population.

What is the basis of such mass support for Communism? In a sense, it is not yet really mass support for Communism as such. Many of those who follow the Communist leadership—probably the vast majority of those who backed the Vietminh in Vietnam —have no idea what Communism is about, nor do they know they are supporting Communists. The backing of the Vietminh in Vietnam was nationalist backing. The Communists in that country skillfully captured control of the anti-French protest movement and, by espousing the cause of nationalist liberation, corralled the supporters who probably made the difference between victory and defeat. The Communists in parts of Indonesia pose as friends of religion; they donate to the construction of mosques and make other contributions to Moslem causes. Their supporters include many sincere Moslems who have no particular affinity for Communism.

There are also a certain number of people anywhere who will jump on the bandwagon once it is rolling. Popular support for the Vietminh grew in Vietnam as the successes of the Ho Chi-minh–led movement became more and more widely known. Surely, also, the strong showing of the Communists in the Indonesian national elections of 1955 encouraged some to vote for the Party in the 1957 provincial and regional elections in Java.

But possibly the greatest long-range danger in Communism's appeal to the masses is that it seeks to capitalize on the disappointment and resentment at the meager returns to date from independence. The nationalist agitators in the years of imperial rule promised improvement of living conditions and other benefits, but the promises have not been kept—as the Communists assiduously point out.

Southeast Asians are learning that people in some parts of the world are very much better off than they are. The masses in the capitalist countries live better, they are told by the Communists, because they achieved their present riches as a result of past colonial exploitation; the masses in the Communist countries live better because this is the way of Communism. Economic contrasts, cleverly exploited, breed resentment. Communism often manages to turn such feelings of resentment to its own advantage.

# Eight

# FOREIGN POLICY

Some leaders of the Southeast Asian nations have had second thoughts about forms of government and domestic policies. But there has been much less change in either foreign-policy objectives or the means employed to fulfill them.

Generally speaking, the foreign-policy aims of the various countries are similar—with the obvious exception of North Vietnam. (As a Communist nation and a satellite of Red China, it must be regarded as sharing the expansionist ambitions of its allies.) The other countries, however, are primarily concerned with maintaining their independence. Most of them are strongly opposed to a major war or any provocative act that could lead to war partly because war (like the arms race among the big nations) would consume resources that might otherwise be used to help them—and partly because of a doctrinaire socialist, anti-colonial identification of war with capitalist rapaciousness. They are devoted to development (meaning essentially modernization) of their national economies. Some of the leaders, in addition, see their nations as playing some kind of role in mediating the differences among the great powers or helping to stabilize the region.

The ends, then, are similar, but the means are often different. It is because of these different means that the countries of Southeast Asia can be said to have divergent foreign policies. These differences apply both to relations with particular nations, such as China, and to approaches to specific problems of foreign policy, such as disarmament. Frequently, there are contradictions between policies toward specific nations and attitudes toward particular subject areas of foreign policy (for example, foreign aid). Let us first survey the policies toward individual nations, then examine approaches to general questions such as colonialism and military alliances.

### Relations with Other Nations

The most important country in the external affairs of all the Southeast Asian nations, even those which do not have diplomatic relations with it, is Communist China. Some of China's southern neighbors were its vassals in one way or another at some time in the past. China's population, estimated to be in excess of 650 million in 1961, is more than three times that of all Southeast Asia, and its total land area is double. Its natural resources are also greater than those of Southeast Asia—particularly coal, iron, and other major ingredients of industrial power. The Chinese Army, increasingly modernized, totals more than 2 million men, and Peking's air force reportedly includes 2,500 combat planes. Moreover, about 15 million persons of distinct Chinese background reside in Southeast Asia today, and well over half of these can be regarded as pro-Peking. The Chinese Communists have the capability to encourage and supply guerrilla wars on their southern flank and will increasingly be able to compete with Japan and the Western countries for markets in Southeast Asia. The big question—both long and short range—is not Peking's capabilities really, but its intentions.

All the Southeast Asian countries, probably including even North Vietnam, fear China. "We fear China so much that we must guard our every word lest we reveal how we truly feel," one former ambassador to Peking from a neutral Southeast Asian country told me. This fear, it should be noted, is not based simply on China's Communist character. Communism only marginally increases the fear.

Burma has consistently followed a policy of conciliation toward Peking, even when Chinese troops crossed into its territory in the mid-1950's. Indonesia has also actively sought to retain

China's friendship, although Sukarno did not back down in 1959 from a diplomatic quarrel with Peking over Indonesia's efforts to restrict the economic activity of foreign nationals, including the Chinese. The Sukarno Government has accepted loan assistance from Peking, as well as from the other Communist countries —and has indicated that it hopes for more help (not less) from both sides in the Cold War. Cambodia, too, has been cordial toward the Chinese Communists; indeed, the Cambodian Government has led the way in accepting aid offers from all quarters in the complicated rivalries of mid-twentieth–century international politics. Prince Norodom Sihanouk was the first non-Communist Southeast Asian political leader to take Chinese credits and technical assistance. Indonesian President Sukarno was next, and Burma's U Nu apparently agreed to accept such aid in the future as a result of Chinese Premier Chou En-lai's visit to Rangoon in early 1961.

Cambodia's troubled neighbor to the north, Laos, has alternately turned an angry and a friendly countenance toward Peking. In late 1960, Prince Souvanna Phouma, then Premier, announced that he was considering recognition of, and aid from, both China and North Vietnam. Subsequently, however, anti-Communist military elements returned to power in the capital of Vientiane (however briefly), and Laos came under heavy attack from the North Vietnamese and Soviets as well as the Chinese. The military victories of the Communist Pathet Lao rebels and their neutralist allies in 1961 probably means that diplomatic relations with China will be inaugurated at some early date. However, this does not mean that the neutralist allies of the Pathets want to become wards of the Chinese. The leading neutralist civilian politician, Prince Souvanna Phouma, is an ardent Laotian nationalist and has said that Communism is not for his country. Whether the neutralists can hold the line against the pro-Communist Pathets is open to serious question.

Only Burma, Indonesia, Cambodia, and North Vietnam, accordingly, had diplomatic ties with the People's Republic of China at the end of 1960. Malaya has no relations with any Chinese government, and the Philippines, Thailand, and South Vietnam recognize the Formosan regime of Chiang Kai-shek.

Singapore, internally self-governing but not yet in control of its external relations, has no direct diplomatic ties with foreign countries.

The reason for this widespread nonrecognition of Peking seems to be the same as that underlying the conciliatory attitude of the Burmese, Indonesians, and Cambodians: fear. Thailand and the Philippines have economically important Chinese minorities, and representatives of the Peking government would be unwelcome for this reason alone. South Vietnam, faced with a Communist threat to its survival by the Chinese-aided North Vietnamese regime, could hardly be expected to show an attitude of cordiality toward Peking. To Malaya, nonrecognition seems the best immediate policy for a country with an unassimilated Chinese minority that accounts for 37 per cent of its population.

Thailand and the Philippines have gone further than merely not recognizing Communist China; they are members of the American-backed SEATO alliance, primarily designed to thwart Chinese aggression. South Vietnam, Laos, and Cambodia are covered by the treaty, although they are not members (partly as a result of restrictions in the 1954 Geneva agreements ending the Indochinese war). South Vietnam has long been a major recipient of United States military aid and advice. The civil war between the Communists and the anti-Communists that made Laos a major point of tension in 1961 prompted not only serious SEATO consideration of military intervention, but also, in a major change of policy, a strong plea by the United States for genuine Laotian neutrality. Although the Geneva Conference that opened in May, 1961, was convened to deal with means to neutralize Laos, it would be dangerously naïve to assume that the Lao can really be insulated from future Chinese influence—given a common frontier, the comparative size of the two countries, Laos' very underdeveloped character, and the nature of Chinese Communism.

Neither South Vietnam nor the Philippines is on particularly good terms with Nationalist China. South Vietnam "nationalized" all Chinese born in the country by declaring them Vietnamese nationals, and the Philippines is involved in almost continuous bickering with Formosa over illegal immigration of Chinese.

Unlike China, India, the other resurgent big nation of Asia, possesses the friendship of practically all the countries of Southeast Asia. The Burmese Government has largely taken its foreign-policy lead from Indian Prime Minister Nehru, and U Nu has sought India's friendship partly as a bulwark against possible future hostile Chinese action. Indonesia also has cooperated actively with India, surprisingly enough in view of its Islamic character and the hostility between the Indians and the Moslem Pakistanis. And Cambodia's Prince Sihanouk has stated on several occasions that he is an admirer and adherent of Indian-style neutralism in foreign relations.

Malaya, Thailand, and the Philippines are on friendly terms with India, but they do not follow India's lead in foreign policy. They also know that India does not approve of some of their pro-Western policies, and this colors their own relationship with the Indians. South Vietnam, indeed, made no effort to disguise its hostility toward India over the manner in which it discharged its responsibilities as chairman of the International Control Commission set up to oversee implementation of the 1954 Geneva settlement. Laos has been generally friendly toward India, but also disliked India's approach in its armistice commission. Communist North Vietnam has sought Indian friendship and received a measure of it, though probably not as much as desired.

The fear of China that seems present everywhere in Southeast Asia is nowhere duplicated respecting India. Such an attitude of trust is, of course, warranted by India's actions to date; but there is a certain naïveté in the widely accepted belief that tomorrow's India will necessarily follow the enlightened policies of today's India.

The only other major Asian nation, Japan, is still in the process of restoring its once friendly image. Before World War II, the Japanese were regarded as potential liberators of the colonial peoples of the area from the yoke of Western domination. During the war, however, Japan proved to be a worse imperial master than the Europeans.

Since the war, the Southeast Asian nations have been indifferent toward Japan. The Japanese are not really liked anywhere in Southeast Asia today, except possibly in Thailand, a wartime ally, but they are not feared either. The major Southeast Asian governments approached a reviving Japan for reparations for war-time damages. Burma was the first to settle with the Japanese on the reparations question, only to feel cheated when the Philippines and Indonesia struck better bargains. The Burmese and the Japanese engaged in further negotiations, and adjustments were made that pleased neither party. South Vietnam has also reached a reparations agreement with Japan, but the Japanese have turned a deaf ear to North Vietnam's claims.

All the countries except North Vietnam now have diplomatic relations with Japan, but Japanese influence in the region does not compare with India's. The Japanese are regaining their former economic position, however, and their goods and technicians are again spreading throughout the area. Their political influence is expected to grow in time, too.

The non-Asian power with the most active relations with the Southeast Asian countries is the United States. This American interest is a development of the years since World War II and a reflection of the world-wide political and security concerns of the U.S. Government. American awareness of Southeast Asia was late in developing, though, and this causes resentment among some Southeast Asian leaders who think that the United States is interested only in using the area in its global Cold War with the Communists.

In the early postwar years, the United States contented itself with a passive role in the affairs of Southeast Asia, but it soon became more interested in the region when China fell to Mao Tse-tung's Communists. Belatedly (or so the Indonesians feel), the American Government brought pressure to bear on the Netherlands to give independence to its Dutch East Indies colony. An economic- and technical-assistance agreement was signed by the United States and Indonesia in 1950. Aid programs were also inaugurated in Thailand and Burma in the same year.

Communist gains in the Vietnamese civil war in 1953–54 forced the United States to increase its financial support of the French military effort against the rebels. The partition of Vietnam into Communist and non-Communist states in 1954 provided the springboard for the establishment of the anti-Communist SEATO alliance. Since that time, the United States has continued its programs of military, financial, and technical assistance to those countries that have needed and would accept such aid. American aid was the main economic support of South Vietnam, Laos, and Cambodia during the second half of the 1950's.

The Philippines and Thailand have been the two Southeast Asian nations most friendly to the United States, both encouraging the American Government to an even more active interest in the area. Both joined the SEATO pact at the time of its inauguration in 1954. The founding conference was held in Manila, and the headquarters subsequently set up in Bangkok. The Philippine friendship for the United States has its roots in a benevolent American colonial policy and American economic assistance following independence. The two countries signed a mutual-defense treaty in 1951. Thailand, a wartime enemy of the United States (so proclaimed, but never recognized by the American Government), has sought American friendship primarily as protection against the Communist Chinese.

There are points of friction, of course, between the United States and these two countries, but they give no present indication of altering the fact or basic character of the friendship. American-Filipino differences have involved the questions of jurisdiction over U.S. forces stationed in the Philippines and continuance of equal investment opportunities for Americans. Despite on-again-off-again negotiations, neither issue has so far been resolved. The main problem of U.S.-Thailand relations concerns Thai resentment over the amount of American economic (and other) aid given such countries as Cambodia and Laos, which do not support the United States diplomatically in the way Thailand does. One Thai official, in a conversation with the author in Bangkok in 1959, characterized his government's attitude: "We ought to get more aid than a neutralist country like Cambodia or a 'semineutral' like Laos." President Kennedy's aid proposals to the American Congress in May, 1961, indicated that the United States had examined the nature of its aid policies and would be more discriminating in the future in the disposition of its assistance, keeping in mind the use made of its financial and technical help—including, in particular, social reforms.

South Vietnam and Malaya also have been particularly

friendly with the United States. American aid enabled South Vietnam to survive amidst the confusion following the 1954 Geneva settlement. Malaya, on the other hand, has not sought the friendship of the United States for the sake of either its political or economic survival, but as part of a general policy of good will toward the major Western nations, including its own former colonial ruler, the United Kingdom.

The remaining non-Communist lands—Burma, Indonesia, and Cambodia—while not hostile to the United States, have been visibly guarded in their relations with it. The orientation of Laos toward the United States has varied with its seemingly ever-changing political complexion, but between 1954 and 1960 it was essentially pro-American in outlook. During these years, the American Government contributed $40 million annually to the Laotian budget.

Of the neutralist countries, Burma probably has been the most friendly to the United States. However, a certain aloofness has characterized the Burmese attitude toward the American Government. The Burmese terminated U.S. aid in 1953, largely as a reaction to American ambivalence concerning Chinese Nationalist irregulars fighting against the Burmese Government. However, Burma strongly fears China, and its leadership appreciates American concern for its fate.

Cambodia, on the other hand, has willingly accepted American economic and technical assistance, but does not appear to be as aware of the Chinese threat as Burma. Indonesia is certainly alert to this threat, but it also imagines a general Western threat to its continued independence and, as a result, has pursued a usually correct but cool policy toward the United States. Communist North Vietnam, of course, has joined China in classifying the United States as "public enemy number one" in the Far East.

Of all nations, the country most disliked by Indonesia is neither the Soviet Union nor China, but its former colonial overlord, the Netherlands. As part of the terms of the 1949 settlement that resulted in Dutch recognition of Indonesian independence, the new island nation agreed to "organized cooperation" with the Dutch through a Netherlands-Indonesian Union. This was supposed to have been a sort of little Dutch "commonwealth." The

Indonesians felt that the 1949 Hague Conference had not settled the question of possession of the western half of the large island of New Guinea (which lies between their land and Australia), thus permitting the Dutch to save face and get legislative approval of the independence agreement. This turned out not to be the case, however, and the Dutch refused even to negotiate on the subject after 1952.* This made the whole Round Table Agreement of 1949 meaningless to Indonesia. Sukarno subsequently unilaterally repudiated it and the financial obligations assumed under it. West Irian, as the Indonesians call western New Guinea, is officially regarded today as the country's number-one foreign-policy problem.

Although the revolt against French rule in Indochina was as bitter as the Indonesian struggle with the Netherlands, the legacy of resentment is not nearly so great. Friendly relations do not exist between North Vietnam and France, but French relations with South Vietnam are cordial.

The United Kingdom is still an influence in Southeast Asia. Its friends are essentially the same as those of the United States. The British retain governing responsibility for the three Borneo territories of North Borneo, Brunei, and Sarawak and have charge of the foreign and defense policies of internally self-governing Singapore. In addition, Malaya is an active member of the Commonwealth, and British as well as Australian and New Zealand troops played a major role in putting down Malaya's Communist rebellion. The relations between Burma and Britain are not as cordial as those between the Malayans and their one-time colonial ruler, but they are friendly. The Burmese, who chose not to join the Commonwealth, accepted British military advisers until 1953.

Perhaps the most important post-independence service rendered Southeast Asia by the British (or, more accurately, the Commonwealth) has been the inauguration and leadership of

---

* There is really no reason to believe that negotiations would have accomplished anything in view of Indonesia's demand for outright cession—and nothing less. The Dutch, for their part, seemed increasingly determined to give the West Irians independence rather than acquiesce in transfer of the territory to the Indonesians.

the Colombo Plan (for the economic development of South and Southeast Asia), which has its headquarters in the capital city of Ceylon. Launched in 1950 at a meeting of Commonwealth foreign ministers, the Colombo Plan now includes among its participants all the countries of Southeast and South Asia except North Vietnam. It is really less a plan than a means whereby nations with the ability to extend aid can ascertain the needs of other countries and endeavor to assist them. Annual conferences are held as part of the process of determining the most pressing needs and assessing the economic development of the area. The United States and the non-Asian Commonwealth countries, including, of course, the United Kingdom itself, are also members.

There are no other Western nations with which the Southeast Asian countries are involved in a significant way, with the possible exception of Australia. Australia shares Commonwealth membership with Malaya and Singapore, is a member of SEATO, and is an important participant in the Colombo Plan. It also governs the eastern half of New Guinea and is a neighbor of Indonesia. Relations between the two nations have been surprisingly good despite Australia's lack of support for Indonesia in the West Irian controversy. New Zealand also is a Commonwealth and SEATO member and has contributed troops to Malaya to fight the Communists. Other Western countries, especially West Germany, have growing economic ties with the area.

The remaining European power with a major interest in Southeast Asia is the Soviet Union. The U.S.S.R.'s direct involvement in the political affairs of the area began in earnest in 1920, when the Indonesian Communist Party joined the Comintern. There was no Soviet governmental contact with any of these countries before World War II, of course, because they were under colonial rule. The U.S.S.R. did not even maintain relations with independent Thailand.

Six states in Southeast Asia now have diplomatic relations with Soviet Russia: North Vietnam, Burma, Indonesia, Cambodia, Laos, and Thailand. When Burma, Indonesia, and Cambodia achieved independence, they recognized the U.S.S.R. in line with their neutralist attitude of being friends with everybody. Laos did not establish diplomatic relations with Russia until

1960, and its recognition then grew out of the internal struggle for power that had engulfed the country. Thailand only recognized the U.S.S.R. in 1946 to ensure its own admission to the United Nations. North Vietnam obviously has close ties with the Soviet Union, but, perhaps significantly, did not seek diplomatic recognition from the U.S.S.R. until late in the colonial war with the French—despite its claim to be an independent government.

Soviet interest in Southeast Asia was minimal immediately after World War II. The Russians were busy recovering from the war and were preoccupied with developments in China. The Communist revolts that broke out in 1948 in various Southeast Asian countries were consistent with changes in international Communist policy concerning the Party's role in such lands. Since the 1954 Geneva settlement, the Soviets have provided major economic support for the North Vietnamese Communists. The U.S.S.R. also inaugurated various types of financial and technical aid to non-Communist countries in the latter half of the 1950's. The Soviets are probably less trusted than the United States; on the other hand, they are not feared in the way that Communist China is.

The relationship between Soviet and Chinese policies toward Southeast Asia is curious. It is difficult to say whether this is the intended result of clever strategy or a reflection of the ideological and other differences between these two powers that were so vigorously expressed at the 1960 Bucharest and Moscow conferences. The Soviet airlift of supplies to the Communist Pathet Lao rebels and their "neutralist" allies in the first months of 1961 seemed odd in view of the fact that the Chinese, who assisted the Vietminh in Vietnam in 1953 and 1954, share a frontier with Laos. The Soviet aircraft, flying from Hanoi, the North Vietnamese capital, also dropped paratroopers to harass advanced positions of the Laotian Army. The Chinese, who have long attacked "the puppets of the imperialists" in Laos, did not get around to threatening military intervention until several weeks after the Soviet-supplied rebel buildup had reached major proportions.

Several explanations were suggested for the apparent Soviet predominance in support of the Laotian Communist insurgents.

Some saw the major role played by the U.S.S.R. as part of a deliberate policy designed to confuse the adversaries of Communism. But others interpreted it as a further illustration of the reportedly growing differences between the two major Communist states. The Soviet Union, they said, was seeking to regain control of the Laotian situation in order to keep the more belligerent Chinese from plunging the world into full-scale war. This was a curious interpretation in view of what seemed to be Soviet efforts to enlarge the scope of the struggle in Laos through its supply of the anti-government elements. Finally, some viewed the actions of the U.S.S.R. as a deliberate move to convince Peking (and others) that it had not gone soft as a revolutionary power and to maintain its position as leader of the world-wide Communist movement. The fact remains, however, that it was the U.S.S.R. which took the lead in supplying and generally supporting the Laotian rebels, and this could not help but be observed by the various interested parties.

There are, of course, major policy differences between the Soviet Union and China. These involve such questions as the inevitability of war, the encouragement of local wars, the achievement of socialism without violence, the desirability of communes, and the role of "peaceful coexistence" as a temporary tactical device or as an end in itself. The U.S.S.R. has taken a softer public line on these matters than China, and it had to face vigorous criticism from the Chinese at the meetings of the world-wide Communist parties in late 1960. The Moscow declaration of December, 1960, represented a triumph for the Soviet point of view, but many regarded the victory as a hollow one.

The role of these two leading Communist states in the 1961 crisis over Laos suggests first that, whatever their motivations, the immediate objectives of the two powers seemed to be the same: prevention of Laos from becoming stronger internally and more closely allied with the Western democratic nations. Second, there apparently has not yet been any division of spheres of influence within the Communist bloc that might give the Chinese undisputed priority in directing Communist activity in Southeast Asia. China, however, might increasingly serve as the chief Communist spokesman in dealing with this area—partly because it is an Oriental country that, like various other lands, has only recently thrown off the yoke of Western domination. There is a kind of affinity for China for just this reason—in addition to the prevalent fear of her.

As the 1955 Bandung Conference showed, the states of Southeast Asia have a strong desire to get to know the other newly independent nations of the world. Indonesia, Burma, Malaya, and Cambodia in particular have sought closer relations with such countries, primarily within the United Nations.

Nevertheless, diplomatic ties with the other new nations are limited. Most of the foreign embassies in the Southeast Asian lands represent Western or Communist countries, and it is in these same countries that Southeast Asians have the major portion of their own overseas representation. Indeed, some of them did not even exchange diplomatic representatives with many of their neighbors in the area until several years after independence. There are various reasons for this failure to exchange more representatives with other newly independent countries. It is expensive, and not all the Southeast Asian countries regard their immediate neighbors or other newly independent countries as important enough to warrant the outlay. In addition, commercial ties and various political needs dictate relations with the older states, while political contact with new nations can be made at the United Nations, in tours abroad by premiers and presidents, and at conferences such as the one at Bandung. Indonesia's cordial relations with other Moslem nations and Burma's ties with Ceylon and Israel are exceptions. Significantly, at the beginning of 1961, there was no representation in or from the new nations of Africa, despite the abundance of good will toward the African countries.

Relations among the countries of Southeast Asia themselves are probably generally better today than at any time since the coming of independence, but there are still important policy differences, as well as serious points of friction, separating some of these nations. North and South Vietnam are proclaimed foes, each allied with one of the two opposing camps in the Cold War and hopeful of ultimate reunification of the land on its own terms. Cambodia, a neutralist country, has charged the neighboring

Thai and South Vietnamese with hostile acts against its territory, partly a projection of the fears of the pre-French period when both these peoples were expanding at the expense of the Cambodians. Various Laotian governments have accused the Communist North Vietnamese of interference in the internal affairs of the country—a charge that seemed clearly substantiated by support accorded the Pathet Lao rebels in the 1961 civil war in that besieged land.

Some of the differences between Southeast Asian countries derive from ties with nations or groups of nations outside the area. Burma, for example, has particularly close relations with Israel and fought (unsuccessfully) for Israeli representation at the 1955 Bandung Conference, while Indonesia's attitude on the Arab-Israeli question is colored by its ties with its sister Islamic nations of the Middle East.

Although the post-independence years have witnessed the re-emergence of such historical antagonisms as those dividing the Thai and the Cambodians, there are other countries that have recently moved closer together. Thai-Burmese relations have become quite cordial since the mid-1950's, despite differing attitudes toward the Cold War, and new ties have developed between Malaya and the Philippines. The Diem Government in South Vietnam—regarded skeptically by some of the Southeast Asian countries in its early years following partition—is more widely accepted today, and even Burma's neutralist U Nu has visited Saigon.

Most of the Southeast Asian lands strongly support the United Nations, which, with its theoretical premise of the sovereign equality of all nations, gives these countries a feeling of importance that they could not get by any other diplomatic means at their disposal. At the United Nations, Burma, for example, and the United States (or the Soviet Union) each has only a single vote in the General Assembly. The big powers, of course, can use their influence to garner the support of other nations, but the smaller countries can seek to match them by the weight of their numbers.

The Southeast Asian countries have also used the United Nations as a means to accomplish particular diplomatic goals.

Indonesia has tried—and failed (with some resulting bitterness)—to obtain U.N. backing for its position in its quarrel with the Dutch over western New Guinea. Burma, too, was disappointed when the U.N. did not throw its full weight on her side in the question of "aggression" by Chinese Nationalist troops.

### Approaches to Major Problems

Probably the only subject on which all the Southeast Asian lands agree is anticolonialism. They are so opposed to continued Western domination of other parts of the world that they seek an end to the remnants of European imperialism wherever they exist. Indonesia, for example, has been a leader in the anticolonial agitation of the Afro-Asian bloc at the United Nations, and not entirely because of its own aspirations for western New Guinea.

Fear of colonialism has clearly colored the approach of some of the Southeast Asian leaders toward foreign aid, and the U.S.-supported Southeast Asian treaty alliance. Indonesia indicated that it feared SEATO as a possible means of interference in its sovereign affairs. Burma apparently gave SEATO more serious consideration than Indonesia and then rejected membership, not only because it did not meet the criteria of its neutralist foreign policy (or because India's Nehru requested such rejection), but also because of a fear (even among informed elements) of a revival of Western colonialism. American economic aid has been regarded with some suspicion by both the Indonesians and the Burmese for much the same reason: a fear that this might be the beginning of an economic imperialism. The "no strings attached" requirement for acceptance of U.S. aid has its roots as much in such feelings as in Cold War neutralism.

This vigorous anticolonialism, which expresses itself in so many different ways, basically reflects two important attitudes: a feeling of injustice and a sense of inferiority. Malaya's strong opposition to South Africa's apartheid racialist policy at the 1960 London meeting of the Commonwealth prime ministers stemmed partly from a belief that this policy was unjust, but it was also probably rooted in Malayan identification with apartheid's victims.

Considering the past expansion of Soviet-directed Communism and the U.S.S.R.'s prediction of an ultimate world-wide triumph of Communism, it is surprising that there is not greater suspicion of the Russians as future colonial oppressors. The United States is regarded as less likely to start a war intentionally or otherwise create trouble for the rest of the world than the Soviets, but, paradoxically, nations like Indonesia, Cambodia, and Burma fear American intervention more than possible Soviet action. The reason for this is not hard to find. The United States was once a colonial power in the area and is a major ally of the former colonial rulers (Britain, France, and the Netherlands). It is a question essentially of fearing the devil one knows—or his friend —and of taking the new devil less seriously. It is still surprising, however, that the U.S.S.R. has not been charged more widely (and vigorously) with interference in Southeast Asian internal affairs as a result of its direction of the indigenous Communist movements in these lands.

Only four of the nations of Southeast Asia seem to be really aware of the menace of international Communism and willing to do something about it. The Philippines and Thailand, both founding members of SEATO, were also the only Southeast Asian countries to send troops to Korea. South Vietnam has accepted American aid and built up its army against the Communists; it is not a member of SEATO only because the Geneva settlement precluded its participation in any such alliance. Malaya has not joined SEATO apparently because Prime Minister Tengku Abdul Rahman finds sufficient protection against Communist aggression in the defense and military assistance treaty with Britain, which is, of course, a leading SEATO member. Malaya has been outspoken about the dangers of Communism, however, and there is no question about where she stands.

The other countries—except, of course, North Vietnam—have adopted a position that assumes, for all practical purposes, the moral equality of American and Soviet intentions. The world has dubbed this as "neutralism," but not all its practitioners like the label. Indonesia describes itself as following "an active independent policy." Burma has noted that it is not neutral, but that at the same time it is not committed in advance to support of a particular nation or bloc. Cambodia's Prince Sihanouk claims that his country wants to be friends with everybody. Laos was formally committed most of the time after the 1954 Geneva settlement to a neutralist course in international politics, but it leaned far more in the direction of the United States during the period 1955-60. Its army—indeed, its whole government—was financially supported by America during these years. However, the civil war of 1960-61—and its results—made adoption of a genuinely neutralist foreign policy virtually a prerequisite for the survival of Laos as even a nominally independent country.*

In theory, the neutralist attitude is an attractive and defensible one. Morally, it is highly meritorious to judge each issue on its own worth as it arises. But practically, there are problems. If the thesis of an international Communist conspiracy directed against the rest of the world is accepted, as it generally is in the West, then neutralism, which is basically unilateralist, in effect gives an edge to the Communists as a result of the disorganized ranks of those they wish to attack, subvert, or otherwise overcome. And since the Soviet Union long ago gave up the prospect of winning any non-Communist Southeast Asian state as the kind of genuine ally that the Philippines and Thailand are of America, neutralism—or the neutralization of possible associates of the Western democratic nations—has become a major objective of Soviet foreign policy. The Indonesians, Burmese, and Cambodians are not pro-Communist because they are neutralist, but their neutralism does aid the Communists.

There is a definite correlation between the degree of anti-Western suspicion and neutralist orientation, on the one hand, and the receptivity to various types of foreign aid, on the other. Thailand, never a colony, and the Philippines are perhaps the least anti-Western. The Thai have not only accepted American economic aid, but have sought more in view of their support of U.S. foreign policy. The Philippines is anti-Western only in a very limited sense and is certainly not neutralist, regarding itself (too

* Whether such neutrality could be effected was the problem facing the fourteen-nation Geneva conference on Laos that opened in May, 1961. The possibility of absorption by the Communist bloc seemed more likely to some observers than neutralization.

smugly, some of its neighbors feel) as an outpost of democracy in Southeast Asia. The Philippines has also asked for more American help than it has received. South Vietnam, which owes its survival as a state to American aid, is, of course, vigorously anti-Communist.

Indonesia supports multilateral economic and technical assistance through the United Nations (of which South Vietnam is not yet a member, for Cold War reasons) as an alternative to potentially compromising unilateral aid programs. The Philippines and Thailand, however, seek both types of aid. Malaya has so far received only limited help from the United States, but not because of suspicion on either side. None of these four countries receives foreign aid from the Soviet Union or any other Communist country.

Cambodia, Indonesia, and Burma, true to neutralist doctrine, have accepted assistance from both sides, although the Burmese also have reneged on acceptance of certain Soviet offers of technical and material help for projects that turned out to involve too heavy a Burmese expenditure of local currency for labor and other costs. Indonesia, apparently more suspicious of the United States than of the U.S.S.R., receives more aid from the Soviets, the Eastern European satellites, and China, than from the American Government and has entered into many trading agreements with the Communists. Its army chief of staff went to Moscow in January, 1961, and successfully negotiated an agreement for the purchase of enough military equipment to double (allegedly) the effective strength of Indonesia's armed forces.

Burma at one time accepted direct American assistance, but called for its cessation in 1953 in connection with the operation of Chinese Nationalist irregulars on Burmese soil. Premier U Nu and his associates, apparently less suspicious of (or less annoyed with) the Communists, accepted Soviet aid offered during the 1955 Khrushchev-Bulganin visit to the country—to be repaid with a "gift" of rice. Burma also turned to the Communists—the Soviets, Eastern Europeans, and Chinese—to get rid of its surplus rice in the middle-1950's, but was not generally pleased with the bargain. Loan assistance by the United States to Burma was subsequently inaugurated instead of the former direct-grant program.

Neutralism has been a positive political force in at least one important sense: its willingness to seek to reconcile the big powers.

Burma's U Nu tried unsuccessfully to bring about a Sino-American *rapproachement* during his 1954 trip to Peking and 1955 visit to the United States. Indonesian President Sukarno, perhaps for varied reasons, was one of the sponsors of the defeated 1960 U.N. General Assembly resolution requesting an Eisenhower-Khrushchev meeting.

Indonesia and Burma have also taken strong stands on behalf of disarmament and an end to nuclear-weapons testing. At the same time, these (and other) countries clearly recognize that the Cold War has created a favorable climate for obtaining economic aid from both sides; thus, they can be said to have a vested interest in its continuation. The Philippines and Thailand have been less than enthusiastic about disarmament, presumably because they share the American suspicion of the Communist position on this issue. North Vietnam, of course, has sounded all the Communist slogans on disarmament at one time or another. Nevertheless, all Southeast Asian countries have significantly increased the size of their defense establishments and more adequately armed their own military forces in recent years.

The main role of the armed forces in Burma and Indonesia is to help maintain internal security. This does not mean that the Burmese and Indonesian armies would not seek to defend their lands against external aggression; it simply reflects the fact that the threat of the independence years has so far been more internal than external. Actually, none of the Southeast Asian countries, neutralist or pro-SEATO, could defend itself for any period against a major foe without outside help. The Philippines and Thailand, SEATO members, expect that help to come mainly from the alliance, particularly from the United States. They seem to regard the treaty as a guarantee that the American Government would come quickly to their aid in the event of Communist military action against them; they also obviously hope that such knowledge will discourage such an attack. The SEATO machinery is not automatic, however. The treaty declares that "each party recognizes that aggression by means of armed attack

in the treaty area . . . would endanger its own peace and safety."
But it also states that each member "will . . . act to meet the
common danger in accordance with its constitutional processes."

Collective defense is the only means available to the neutralist
countries for resisting aggression, and these countries know this.
The Burmese, who have already sought U.N. action against
aggression from Chinese Nationalist irregulars, have frequently
acknowledged their dependence on U.N.-style collective security.
Laos and Cambodia also have made such acknowledgments.
Indonesia, sensitive and hesitant to indicate too strongly its reliance on any external source, does recognize its dependence on
the United Nations in this respect.

There were a variety of proposals for intraregional cooperation
in the wake of World War II, but none of these ever got off the
ground. The Philippines, before the war, proposed a pan-Malay
union for closer cooperation among the ethnically related peoples
of insular Southeast Asia. Post-colonial Philippine presidents
ambitiously suggested various broader associations concerned
with defense, economics, or whatever subjects might be of interest
to potential participants. These would have covered all of Southeast Asia—and South and East Asia as well. However, such efforts
bore no real fruit.

Malaya is quite favorably oriented toward closer regional
cooperation, although it has no intention of joining SEATO. The
Alliance Government has sought to encourage closer general
cooperation, particularly economically, among the countries of
the area through its proposal for an Association of Southeast
Asian States. This would involve agreement, in effect, to consult
wherever possible; and the Malayans hope that out of such
consultations some firmer institutional forms of cooperation, such
as a regional customs union, might emerge. The ASAS would
have no military character, however. The Philippines and Thailand have strongly endorsed the Malayan initiative, and the
three states are actively consulting concerning establishment of
such an organization. South Vietnam, Burma, and Laos (prior
to its civil war) have shown interest (particularly the first country); Cambodia has not revealed much concern one way or the
other, and Indonesia is clearly opposed. Cambodia and Laos, as

well as Thailand, have also shown some interest in the past in a Buddhist bloc, although there have not been any recent proposals of this sort.

In general, Indonesia has been the least interested of the countries of Southeast Asia in any form of regional cooperation, and it is followed by Burma, Cambodia, and Laos. Although they vigorously deny it, this has partly been a reflection of an isolationist tendency in these countries, particularly Indonesia and Burma. These nations also prefer to utilize other organizations, such as the U.N., in those circumstances where cooperation is warranted.

The Philippines, Malaya, Thailand, and South Vietnam are less sensitive about infringement on their freedom of action through regional cooperation, and more realistic, perhaps, about the benefits of such associations. It is interesting that the neutralist nations and the anti-Communist countries should line up together on different sides on the general question of regional cooperation.

All the Southeast Asian countries more or less regularly consult with other nations—mostly those outside Southeast Asia. The Philippines, somewhat of a lone wolf among Asian countries despite its pro-regional orientation, consults regularly with the United States on all major foreign-policy questions. Thailand consults more with the United States than it does with any other power, but not as closely as the Philippines does. The same can be said of South Vietnam and Laos (when the Laotian Government has been pro-Western, as contrasted with neutralist). Cambodia has not really shown any inclination toward regular consultation with other countries at any time.

Burma has cooperated particularly closely with its neighbor India, and, on a much broader basis, with various other leading Afro-Asian nations. There are close economic and political ties, also, between the Burmese and such contrasting countries as Yugoslavia and Israel—but Burma would not consult on general policy questions with these countries. Indonesia, although more disposed toward general consultation with India than any other country except Burma, tends more to discuss policy alternatives with all the leading members of the Afro-Asian group at the United Nations. Malaya has so far consulted more with its former colonial ruler, the United Kingdom, than anybody else, although it has shown an increasing tendency to confer with various Afro-Asian countries, particularly Commonwealth ones and the Philippines. North Vietnam is a Southeast Asian edition of the usual satellite association with a major Communist power or powers.

The pattern of this "tendency to consult," if such it may be called, suggests much larger American than Soviet or Chinese influence. The Philippines, Thailand, and South Vietnam seek at least to inform the United States of major decisions in the process of formation. Only North Vietnam appears closely associated with China or the Soviet Union. The influence of the United States in even the neutralist countries seems to equal or surpass that of the Communists. This is true despite the fact that their neutralist policies seem to favor the Communists.

\*    \*    \*

Foreign policies and patterns of international behavior have not yet become solidified in Southeast Asia. But they are consistent enough to be predictable. The countries of Southeast Asia can be grouped loosely into three categories: those most likely to make basic foreign-policy changes in the near future, those least likely to do so, and those somewhere in the middle.

North Vietnam, the Philippines, and Thailand seem least likely to undergo early foreign-policy changes. Laos, with serious internal dissension, is probably the country that could become more Communist-oriented in the shortest time. South Vietnam, where conflicting views on foreign and other policies are currently suppressed and where Communist infiltrators continue to bore away, and Cambodia, so dependent on the whims of a single man, could hardly be called stable in terms of probable future persistence of present foreign policies.

Burma, Malaya, and Indonesia form a middle-ground corps of countries whose foreign policies are likely to change more than those of the first group, but less than those of the last.

Changes, if they come, will probably result primarily from external pressures beyond the immediate control of the individual governments. Although Laotian conservative regimes caused a great deal of their own trouble in 1960-61, neither they—nor their Communist adversaries—could end the difficulties by themselves. This was the objective and significance of the fourteen-nation Geneva conference on Laos in 1961. The goal of the United States and its allies (including the Laotian conservatives) —one that was painfully decided upon—was neutralization of the country. The differences between the Communists and anti-Communists probably did not concern the form of neutralization at all. China's Mao Tse-tung long ago said that there could be no neutrality in the historic struggle between Communism and capitalism, and Communist intermediate policies must be judged accordingly.

The important point is that change is likely in Laotian foreign policy, and that other powers will really be the ones to determine finally the degree—and duration—of that change. There is a lesson here for those who sit in positions of political authority in all the lands of Southeast Asia—a lesson that might suggest significant policy changes toward Communism, the United States, and the United Nations, and closer regional political (and military) collaboration. It remains to be seen whether the lesson will be learned.

NINE

# FACING THE FUTURE

THE FIRST years of political independence in Southeast Asia served to get the new nations started. Even long-independent Thailand had to make a new start in a world of other free non-European states with new values and new dimensions.

The foundations of statehood having been laid, the decade of the 1960's started out as one of adjustments in governmental structures and national policies. Critics inside and outside these countries will find fault with the adjustments, but, after all, this is a time of change in Southeast Asia and elsewhere in the former colonies, and if today's readjustments do not prove to be the answer, tomorrow's may do the trick. Burma's survival proves that a nation can make quite a few mistakes, reach the brink of disaster several times, and still pull through.

It is true that only the Philippines, Malaya, Singapore, and Burma have democratically elected governments today, but in the last few centuries there has been a growing participation of total populations in the political process the world over (Communism notwithstanding), and in time popular government will probably be the rule rather than the exception in Southeast Asia.

However, democratic government will not come about without revolutionary changes in the politics of Southeast Asia. The transition from the European colonial period to freedom was a gigantic step. It is now necessary to carry these countries out of their present economically underdeveloped and politically unsettled stage—even at the risk of undemocratic governments in the short run. This is a risk, however—and not a requirement.

There is a moral quality to democracy that is widely recognized in the United States and Europe, but it should also be remembered that democracy is an extremely practical means of resolving conflict. However, this is more apparent in societies that are comparatively developed economically. There is admittedly a certain appeal to the authoritarian approach in modernizing backward economies, but there is also a strong attractiveness to democracy once the modernization process has taken place. This is not to say that authoritarian government is preferable to democratic rule in uplifting backward countries, but rather that democracy seems both more appropriate and more necessary in developed than in underdeveloped countries.

Probably the least painful way for the countries of Southeast Asia to effect both economic modernization and accompanying political development is through acceptance of help from abroad. With democratic or semidemocratic governments like those of Malaya, the Philippines, or Burma, the nations of this part of the world could transform their economies without resort to dictatorial regimes (which, once established and however useful in certain circumstances, are notoriously difficult to get rid of). Economic modernization and diversification could stimulate the creation of groups that might regard democratic political procedures as the most practical means of reconciling their differences. Foreign aid has been given in the past for political purposes, and it could be given in the future with a conscious eye on the internal political consequences of diversified economic groups.

Economic aid from the Soviet Union and other Communist and totalitarian countries, rather than posing a threat to the continued free existence of the Southeast Asian nations, could help considerably in the task of economic modernization and diversification. Such aid could prove the difference between success or failure for a democratically devised five-year plan. It has too frequently been felt in the past that acceptance of such help was the first step toward Communist control, but the fact that the U.S.S.R. hopes to win influence by this means is no guarantee that it will succeed.

The threat of Communism to Southeast Asia today stems primarily from the indigenous Communist parties and from China. The first danger—that of a takeover by local Communists through one means or another—is the more likely. It is also the more difficult to combat. Strong-arm governments able to keep local Communists in check also generate the kind of resentment on which Communism thrives. Progress in economic development and in other areas, measures to eliminate or reduce discontent, mild repression where necessary (but *only* where necessary), and, above all, dedication and political skill on the part of the non-Communists seem to be the only real means of effectively preventing internal Communist seizures.

A direct attack by Communist China against any of the Southeast Asian countries seems improbable. On the other hand, there are many reasons for believing that the Chinese seek ultimately to control by one means or another the rich area to their south. SEATO is one answer to this threat. A more basic approach to the problem might be to influence by some means or another China's image of itself as the necessarily dominant power in South and East Asia, reduce its nationalist resentment and frustration, give it a place in the international community commensurate with its importance, and provide an opportunity for the Chinese to try to coexist with the non-Communist world.

The Chinese or Communist threat, however, is only one of the many problems facing the countries of Southeast Asia. The fact is that while these nations are attempting to make domestic transitions of tremendous proportions, the world around them is also straining at the seams. Adjustment to either situation would be difficult at any time; adjustment to both at once produces tensions that inevitably take their toll.

Southeast Asia requires two things above all else in the immediate years ahead: good leadership, and outside help and understanding. It has received generally good leadership from some of its leaders to date: U Nu and Ne Win in Burma, Tengku Abdul Rahman in Malaya, and the late Ramón Magsaysay in the Philippines. It is difficult to say whether Indonesia's Sukarno or South Vietnam's Diem fall in this category. Though the means they use may not be palatable to many, their kind of leadership may be what is needed at this particular hour in the history of

Southeast Asia. Sukarno has earlier been described as the cause of many of his country's ills, which he is. However, he has also held the nation together in the most trying of times, which no one else might have done.

What good leadership is in emerging lands like those of Southeast Asia is difficult to specify. But it surely must hold the nation together, compensate for the shortcomings of an unsettled or otherwise inadequate political process, and contribute to the development of a stable and maturing governmental system. It is probably more important that such leadership exist than that it be of a particular type. South Vietnam's President Diem will probably be judged in the future not in terms of whether he governed democratically, but whether he saved his country from Communism or disintegration and left Vietnam a better place when his ruling days were over.

As for outside help and understanding, the Communists, the democratic nations, and even the other former colonial states of Asia and Africa each assume too frequently that they alone know what is best for the Southeast Asian countries. Although they may possess some insight stemming from perspective, they probably do not know Burma as well as U Nu, or Indonesia as well as Sukarno. Outside help should be based on more of a working partnership, with both partners showing more mutual understanding than they have up to now.

This should not only make the future easier to face, but also make it a more palatable future for both Southeast Asians and those lands that genuinely aspire to assist them in meeting the problems that face them in such abundance.

# SELECTED BIBLIOGRAPHY

THE LITERATURE dealing with Southeast Asia has grown rapidly in recent years, and it is likely to continue to grow in both quality and quantity. In addition to the books listed below, there are several periodicals of which the reader should be aware. These include the quarterly *Pacific Affairs* (published by the Institute of Pacific Relations), the quarterly *Journal of Asian Studies* (published by the Association for Asian Studies), and the monthly *Asian Survey* (published by the Institute of International Studies of the University of California; this is the successor to the long-reliable *Far Eastern Survey*, which was issued by the Institute of Pacific Affairs and which ceased publication in February, 1961). So many professional journals and other periodicals carry good material from time to time that it is impossible to note them all, but conspicuous in this respect are *Foreign Affairs*, the *American Universities Field Staff Reports*, *The Economist* (London), *The Reporter*, and *The New Leader*. *The New York Times* offers the most detailed press coverage of the area, but the reporting and analysis in *The Christian Science Monitor*, *St. Louis Post-Dispatch*, and *Chicago Daily News* are also very good. Bibliographic material is available from a variety of sources, including the Institute of Pacific Relations (at the University of British Columbia in Vancouver) and the Asia Society (in New York).

## GENERAL

DOBBY, E. H. G. *Southeast Asia*. 6th ed. London: University of London Press, 1958. A standard geography.
DUBOIS, CORA. *Social Forces in Southeast Asia*. Cambridge, Mass.: Harvard University Press, 1959. A reprint of an outstanding work first published in 1949.

EMERSON, RUPERT. *From Empire to Nation: The Rise to Self-Assertion of Asian and African Peoples.* Cambridge, Mass.: Harvard University Press, 1960.

————. *Representative Government in Southeast Asia.* Cambridge, Mass.: Harvard University Press, 1955.

FIFIELD, RUSSELL F. *The Diplomacy of Southeast Asia, 1954–1958.* New York: Harper & Brothers, 1958.

GINSBERG, NORTON (ed.). *The Pattern of Asia.* Englewood Cliffs, N. J.: Prentice-Hall, 1958. The material on Southeast Asia represents the best geographical introduction to the area.

HALL, D. G. E. *A History of South-east Asia.* New York: St Martin's Press, 1955.

HARRISON, BRIAN. *South-east Asia, A Short History.* New York: St. Martin's Press, 1954; London: Macmillan & Co., 1954.

HEINE-GELDERN, ROBERT. *Conceptions of State and Kingship in Southeast Asia.* Ithaca, N. Y.: Southeast Asia Program, Cornell University, 1956.

JACOBY, ERICH H. *Agrarian Unrest in Southeast Asia.* New York: Columbia University Press, 1949.

KAHIN, GEORGE McT. (ed.). *Governments and Politics of Southeast Asia.* Ithaca, N. Y.: Cornell University Press, 1959. An outstanding text.

MILLIKAN, MAX F., and BLACKMER, DONALD L. M. *The Emerging Nations, Their Growth and United States Policy.* Boston: Little, Brown & Co., 1961.

MURDOCK, GEORGE P. (ed.). *Social Structure in Southeast Asia.* Chicago: Quadrangle Books, 1960.

PYE, LUCIAN W. "The Politics of Southeast Asia," in ALMOND, GABRIEL A., and COLEMAN, JAMES S. (ed.). *The Politics of the Developing Areas.* Princeton, N. J.: Princeton University Press, 1960. The interested reader should also look at the introductory and concluding sections of this book.

ROBEQUAIN, CHARLES. *Malaya, Indonesia, Borneo, and the Philippines: A Geographical, Economic, and Political Description of Malaya, the East Indies, and the Philippines.* Translated by E. D. LABORDE. 2nd ed. London and New York: Longmans, Green & Co., 1958. A good regional geography.

ROSE, SAUL. *Socialism in Southern Asia.* New York: Oxford University Press, 1959.

TRAGER, FRANK N. (ed.). *Marxism in Southeast Asia.* Stanford, Calif.: Stanford University Press, 1959.

VANDENBOSCH, AMRY, and BUTWELL, RICHARD. *Southeast Asia Among the World Powers.* Lexington, Ky.: University of Kentucky Press, 1957.

WOLF, CHARLES, JR. *Foreign Aid: Theory and Practice in Southern Asia.* Princeton, N. J.: Princeton University Press, 1960.

## BURMA

CADY, JOHN F. *A History of Modern Burma*. Ithaca, N. Y.: Cornell University Press, 1958. This book provides an outstanding introduction to the country.

FURNIVALL, J. S. *An Introduction to the Political Economy of Burma*. 3rd ed. Rangoon: People's Literature Committee & House, 1957.

————. *Colonial Policy and Practice: A Comparative Study of Burma and Netherlands India*. New York: New York University Press, 1956. A reprint of a classic work.

————. *The Governance of Modern Burma*. New York: Institute of Pacific Relations, 1958. The best study of contemporary politics.

HAGEN, EVERETT E. *The Economic Development of Burma*. Washington: National Planning Association, 1956.

MAUNG MAUNG. *Burma's Constitution*. The Hague: Martinus Nijhoff, 1959. A less technical book than the title suggests; written by an astute Burmese observer.

TINKER, HUGH. *The Union of Burma*. 2nd ed. London and New York: Oxford University Press, 1959.

TRAGER, FRANK N. *Building a Welfare State in Burma*. New York: Institute of Pacific Relations, 1958.

## CAMBODIA

HERZ, MARTIN F. *A Short History of Cambodia*. New York: Frederick A. Praeger, 1958.

STEINBERG, DAVID (ed.). *Cambodia: Its People, Its Society, Its Culture*. Human Relations Area Files. New York: Taplinger Publishing Co., 1959.

## INDONESIA

ALLEN, G. C., and DONNITHORNE, AUDREY G. *Western Enterprise in Indonesia and Malaya*. New York: The Macmillan Co., 1957.

BOEKE, J. H. *Economics and Economic Policy of Dual Societies as Exemplified by Indonesia*. New York: Institute of Pacific Relations, 1953.

FURNIVALL, J. S. *Netherlands India: A Study of Plural Economy*. New York: The Macmillan Co., 1944.

GEERTZ, CLIFFORD. *The Social Context of Economic Change: An Indonesian Case Study*. Cambridge, Mass.: Center for International Studies, Massachusetts Institute of Technology, 1956.

HANNA, WILLARD A. *Bung Karno's Indonesia*. Rev. ed. New York: American Universities Field Staff, 1961.

HIGGINS, BENJAMIN. *Indonesia's Economic Stabilization and Development*. New York: Institute of Pacific Relations, 1957.

KAHIN, GEORGE McT. *Nationalism and Revolution in Indonesia*. Ithaca, N. Y.: Cornell University Press, 1952.

SJAHRIR, SOETAN. *Out of Exile*. Translated by CHARLES WOLF, JR. New York: The John Day Company, 1949. The author is a long-time nationalist and former Prime Minister of Indonesia.

VANDENBOSCH, AMRY. *The Dutch East Indies*. Berkeley, Calif.: University of California Press, 1942. The best survey of the pre–World War II Dutch East Indies.

VLEKKE, BERNARD H. M. *Nusantara: A History of Indonesia*. Rev. ed. Chicago: Quadrangle Books, 1960.

VON NEIL, ROBERT. *The Emergence of the Modern Indonesian Elite*. Chicago: Quadrangle Books, 1960.

WERTHEIM, W. F. *Indonesian Society in Transition: A Study of Social Change*. 2nd ed. The Hague: Van Hoeve, 1959.

## LAOS

FALL, BERNARD B. *Laos: Background of a Conflict*. Washington: Public Affairs Press, 1961.

LeBAR, FRANK M. (ed.). *Laos: Its People, Its Society, Its Culture*. Human Relations Area Files. New York: Taplinger Publishing Co., 1960.

MEEKER, ODEN. *The Little World of Laos*. New York: Charles Scribner's Sons, 1959.

SISOUK NA CHAMPASSAK. *Storm Over Laos: A Contemporary History*. New York: Frederick A. Praeger, 1961.

## MALAYA AND SINGAPORE

EMERSON, RUPERT. *Malaysia: A Study in Direct and Indirect Rule*. New York: The Macmillan Co., 1937.

GINSBURG, NORTON, and ROBERTS, CHESTER F., JR. *Malaya*. Seattle, Wash.: University of Washington Press, 1958.

MILLS, LENNOX A. *Malaya: A Political and Economic Appraisal*. Minneapolis, Minn.: University of Minnesota Press, 1958.

PARKINSON, C. NORTHCOTE. *A Short History of Malaya*. Singapore: Moore, 1954.

PYE, LUCIAN W. *Guerrilla Communism in Malaya: Its Social and Political Meaning*. Princeton, N. J.: Princeton University Press, 1956.

## THE PHILIPPINES

BERNSTEIN, DAVID. *The Philippine Story*. New York: Farrar, Straus & Cudahy, 1947.

CORPUZ, O. D. *The Bureaucracy in the Philippines*. Manila: Institute of Public Administration, University of the Philippines, 1957.

GOLAY, FRANK. *The Philippines: A Study in National Economic Development*. Ithaca, N. Y.: Cornell University Press, 1961.

HARRISON, FRANCIS BURTON. *The Corner-stone of Philippine Independence: A Narrative of Seven Years.* New York: Century, 1922. The author describes the "Filipinization" of the colonial government during the Wilson Administration.

HAYDEN, JOSEPH RALSTON. *The Philippines: A Study in National Development.* New York: The Macmillan Co., 1942. The best pre-independence study.

JACOBINI, H. B., *et al. Governmental Services in the Philippines.* Manila: Institute of Public Administration, University of the Philippines, 1956.

QUIRINO, CARLOS. *Magsaysay of the Philippines.* Manila: Alemars, 1958.

ROMANI, JOHN H. *The Philippine Presidency.* Manila: Institute of Public Administration, University of the Philippines, 1956.

ROMULO, CARLOS P. *Crusade in Asia: Philippine Victory.* New York: The John Day Company, 1955. This book treats the restoration of democratic procedures in the post-Hukbalahap period.

SCAFF, ALVIN H. *The Philippine Answer to Communism.* Stanford, Calif.: Stanford University Press, 1955.

SMITH, ROBERT AURA. *Philippine Freedom, 1946–1958.* New York: Columbia University Press, 1958.

## THAILAND

BLANCHARD, WENDELL, AHALT, HENRY C., *et al. Thailand: Its People, Its Society, Its Culture.* Human Relations Area Files. New York: Taplinger Publishing Co., 1958.

COUGHLIN, RICHARD J. *Double Identity: The Chinese in Modern Thailand.* New York: Oxford University Press, 1961.

DE YOUNG, JOHN E. *Village Life in Modern Thailand.* Berkeley, Calif.: University of California Press, 1955.

INGRAM, JAMES C. *Economic Change in Thailand Since 1850.* Stanford, Calif.: Stanford University Press, 1955.

LANDON, KENNETH PERRY. *Siam in Transition.* Shanghai: Kelly and Walsh, 1939. A good description of Thai politics in the 1930's.

SKINNER, G. WILLIAM. *Chinese Society in Thailand: An Analytical History.* Ithaca, N. Y.: Cornell University Press, 1957.

———. *Leadership and Power in the Chinese Community of Thailand.* Ithaca, N. Y.: Cornell University Press, 1958.

VELLA, WALTER. *The Impact of the West on Government in Thailand.* Berkeley, Calif.: University of California Press, 1955.

## VIETNAM (NORTH AND SOUTH)

BUTTINGER, JOSEPH. *The Smaller Dragon: A Political History of Vietnam.* New York: Frederick A. Praeger, 1958.

FALL, BERNARD B. *The Viet-Minh Regime: Government and Administration in the Democratic Republic of Vietnam.* 2nd ed. New York: Institute of Pacific Relations, 1956.

————. *Street Without Joy.* Harrisburg, Pa.: The Stackpole Co., 1961. An account of revolutionary warfare in Indochina.

HAMMER, ELLEN. *The Struggle for Indochina.* Stanford, Calif.: Stanford University Press, 1954.

LINDHOLM, RICHARD W. (ed.). *Viet-Nam: The First Five Years.* East Lansing, Mich.: Michigan State University Press, 1959.

# INDEX